VIRAL MARKETING

VIRAL MARKETING:
THE SCIENCE OF
SHARING

KAREN NELSON-FIELD
Byron Sharp (Academic Editor)

OXFORD
UNIVERSITY PRESS
AUSTRALIA & NEW ZEALAND

OXFORD
UNIVERSITY PRESS

Oxford University Press is a department of the University of Oxford.

It furthers the University's objective of excellence in research, scholarship, and education by publishing worldwide. Oxford is a registered trademark of Oxford University Press in the UK and in certain other countries.

Published in Australia by
Oxford University Press

253 Normanby Road, South Melbourne, Victoria 3205, Australia

National Library of Australia Cataloguing-in-Publication entry

Author: Nelson-Field, Karen, author.
Title: Viral marketing: the science of sharing/Karen Nelson-Field.
ISBN: 9780195527988 (paperback)
Notes: Includes bibliographical references.
Subjects: Digital communications–Social aspects.
Video recordings–Social aspects.
Computer file sharing–Social aspects.
Information technology–Social aspects.
Interactive computer systems–Social aspects.
Dewey Number: 303.4834

Edited by Pete Cruttenden
Typeset by diacriTech, India
Printed by Ligare

FOREWORD

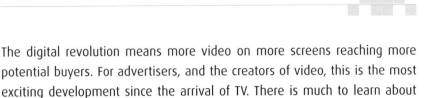

The digital revolution means more video on more screens reaching more potential buyers. For advertisers, and the creators of video, this is the most exciting development since the arrival of TV. There is much to learn about these new media, and much creative thinking that needs to be done, along with well-designed experiments.

A little fundamental knowledge would help thinking in this area enormously. This is what some of the best brains in business—the members of the Advisory Boards of the Ehrenberg-Bass Institute—had in mind when they asked us to start work in social media. 'Identify and clear away the myths,' they instructed. 'Give us something solid on which to build our knowledge and capability.'

Dr Karen Nelson-Field has led this endeavour, working very long days yet remaining enthusiastic. That enthusiasm and commitment attracted her peers and she was able to bring in some great talent, both within the Institute and outside, to help with advice, analysis, alternative hypotheses and explanations, coding, checking and replicating.

The result is this book: this compelling, exciting, solid and ground-breaking research. This is just the start—a foundation on which to develop and refine your digital video advertising strategy. May you learn and prosper from it.

Professor Byron Sharp, author of *How Brands Grow*

PS. During the minute it took for you to read this preface, more than 100 hours of new video has been uploaded to YouTube.

www.MarketingScience.info

CONTENTS

AUTHOR

Dr Karen Nelson-Field is a Senior Research Associate with the Ehrenberg-Bass Institute at the University of South Australia. Her current research focuses on whether existing empirical generalisations in advertising and buyer behaviour hold in the new media context. Her research into social media marketing, content marketing and video sharing has been internationally recognised both in industry and academic forums, while her sometimes controversial findings regularly spark global discussion among practitioners.

Professor Byron Sharp (Academic Editor) is a Professor of Marketing Science and Director of the Ehrenberg-Bass Institute at the University of South Australia. The Institute's research is sponsored by corporations around the world including Coca-Cola, Mars, P&G, Kraft, Turner Broadcasting, CBS and the Australian Research Council. His book *How Brands Grow* (Oxford University Press 2010) presents a wide variety of scientific laws and what they mean for marketing strategy.

www.MarketingScience.info

CONTRIBUTORS

Associate Professor Jenni Romaniuk

Jenni Romaniuk is an Associate Research Professor of Brand Equity and Associate Director (International) of the Ehrenberg-Bass Institute for Marketing Science. She is also a regular columnist in the *Journal of Advertising Research*. Her key areas of research are brand equity, advertising effectiveness, word-of-mouth and customer loyalty. She advises companies around the globe on these issues.

Dr Jennifer Taylor

Jennifer Taylor is a Senior Research Associate and Lecturer in the Ehrenberg-Bass Institute at the University of South Australia. Her key area of research interest and expertise is advertising effectiveness, with a particular focus on single-source measurement.

Nicole Hartnett

Nicole Hartnett is a Senior Research Associate at the Ehrenberg-Bass Institute for Marketing Science at the University of South Australia. Her current research interests centre around measuring advertising effects and advertising creativity.

Dr Erica Riebe

Erica Riebe is a Senior Researcher at the Ehrenberg-Bass Institute at the University of South Australia. Her work focuses on determining effective media placement strategies and measuring the impact of change in the media environment on audiences.

Kellie Newstead

Kellie Newstead is a Research Associate at the Ehrenberg-Bass Institute at the University of South Australia. Her research area is focused on understanding why and how marketing managers make changes to advertising. This includes understanding what effect changes to branding elements in advertising have on consumers' ability to recognise the advertised brand. Her other research interests include new media and media strategy.

Dr Haydn Northover

Haydn Northover has recently completed his PhD thesis, 'Are biometrics better' (fMRI, EEG and skin conductance, among others). Haydn's key research interest is understanding how emotion and memory are measured, particularly in an advertising pre-testing context. Building on 15 years of advertising and communications research for some of the largest market research companies, Haydn has recently launched his own research company, The Ship. Haydn continues to teach at the University of South Australia.

ACKNOWLEDGMENTS

Thank you to the following for their contributions to this text: John Robinson, Rachel Kennedy, Melissa Banelis, Carole Lydon, Pete Hammer and Elke Seretis.

I would like to especially thank Unruly Media for their data contribution, without which this book would not have been possible. In particular, I would like to thank Sarah Wood, Cat Jones, Ian Forrester, Phil Townend and David Waterhouse for their endless hours of discussion, insight and debate.

Thank you also to our corporate sponsors, who share our quest for both useful and rigorous marketing research. Our sponsors include:

AUSTRALASIA, NEW ZEALAND AND ASIA

AkzoNobel Paints

ANZ National Bank

Carlton & United Breweries

Cerebos

Colgate-Palmolive

Department of Environment, Water and Natural Resources

Elders

Fonterra

Foxtel

GlaxoSmithKline

GWRDC

Kmart Australia

KWP! Advertising

Lion Drinks and Dairy

Mars

Mondelez Asia Pacific

People's Choice Credit Union

PHD

Roy Morgan Research

Schweppes Australia

Seafood CRC

The Coca-Cola Company

The Nielsen Company

Unilever

United Spirits Limited

University of South Australia

EUROPE

Britvic

Coca-Cola Great Britain

Colgate-Palmolive

Kantar Worldpanel (Spain)

Kantar Worldpanel (UK)

Kellogg's

Leo Burnett

Mars

Mountainview Learning

Pagen

SABMiller

The Coca-Cola Company

The Edrington Group

The Nielsen Company

Unilever

USA AND CANADA

Advertising Research Foundation

CBS

Colgate-Palmolive

ESPN

General Mills

General Motors

Innerscope Research

Kimberly-Clark

Mondelez International

Procter & Gamble

Sun Products Corporation

The Coca-Cola Company

The Nielsen Company

Turner Broadcasting

Unilever

SOUTH AFRICA

Caxton Publishers and Printers

Colgate-Palmolive

Distell

FirstRand

Finally to Pete, Connor and Alec, thank you for being amazing (and patient).

Karen Nelson-Field, June 2013

www.MarketingScience.info

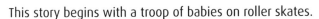

1

IT'S AN EPIDEMIC

KAREN NELSON-FIELD

This story begins with a troop of babies on roller skates.

In 2009, a memorable social video from bottled water brand Evian broke world records for the most viewed online video advertisement in history (*World Record Academy* 2011). 'Evian Roller Babies',[1] featuring break-dancing infants on roller skates, cracked more than 45 million online views worldwide, all from YouTube alone. It was seeded simultaneously across six countries with success measured by high levels of sharing (three million to date), reported sales increases in most regions, and €5m in free airtime, including *Time Magazine* and the *Wall Street Journal* (*This is not Advertising* 2011).

It was one of the first social video campaigns by a major brand and showed marketers that social video, as an alternative to traditional media, has the potential for tremendous advertising reach at a fraction of the cost. So it's no surprise that in the past couple of years the growth of social video[2] as an advertising format has exploded and is showing no signs of abating. In the USA, in December alone, over 11 billion social videos were watched (*comScore* 2013). For a marketer, that is access to a lot of eyeballs. 'Evian Roller Babies'

---

1   Creative and Media Agency: BETC Euro RSCG, Paris; Seeding Agency: Unruly Media.
2   For the most part in this book we refer to online videos as social videos. 'Social video' is the term used for videos produced by marketers that in most cases use paid distribution to kick-start viewership.

is a true viral success. This book employs scientific methods to understand why. It peels back the layers of viral marketing success to understand how to replicate the viral spiral that makes a superstar social video.

Advertisers are becoming increasingly attracted to the possibility that they can create a video advertisement for their brand that will 'go viral' like an infectious disease that spreads to millions from a small base—if the video is infectious enough! But what makes a social video infectious is largely unknown. Meanwhile, many are falling over each other to be the first to 'crack the viral code'. This is resulting in an abundance of opinion pieces and case studies, but a lack of rigorous marketing science on the topic. This, however, is a typical consequence of new media, where change occurs ahead of learning (see Chapter 2):

> Early knowledge is patchy in substance; research findings often are reduced to sound bites that get passed on without any regard to the quality of the underpinning research. Case studies—particularly 'successes'—are taken as gospel instead of being treated more appropriately as single plot points in a larger story. (Romaniuk 2012)

Now four years on, with the viewership of 'Evian Roller Babies' in excess of 100 million, brands are still trying to understand the magic behind its success. While a few successes have followed—for example, Volkswagen's 'The Force', T-Mobile's 'Angry Birds Live', Old Spice's 'The Man Your Man Could Smell Like' and, more recently, Pepsi Max's 'Test Drive'—these are extreme exceptions that are far from the norm. In fact, in Chapter 6 you will see how the vast majority of social videos are little viewed and shared. Only 5 per cent of videos are responsible for over half of all reach, and some marketers are well aware of this plight:

> The potential upside of using social video in the media mix is high: more sales from the deeper emotional effect of videos that reach large numbers of people. The downside is time and effort and money wasted on videos that go nowhere. Most brand videos today are unfortunately in this latter category. (Frank Harrison, Strategic Resources Director Worldwide, ZenithOptimedia)

And while some savvy marketers are cautious of over-investment without rigorous justification, most are seduced by the advertisers' dream—free reach.

> Don't be seduced by new! Technology is there to serve your strategy; your strategy should not serve technology. Rigorously explore new media to enable a better execution of your growth strategy. Any other approach is a gamble with your shareholders' money. (Bruce McColl, Chief Marketing Officer, Mars Inc.)

So what makes 'Evian Roller Babies' a truly viral success? According to Michael Aidan, global brand director of Evian:

> The combination of seeding and posting the film worldwide on YouTube has helped us reach well beyond our expectations: the most viewed video ad on the web ever. Even more spectacular is the spontaneous relay TV channels around the world gave to this 'web sensation' and the 350 equally spontaneous remixed versions of the spot that have now reached millions. (*Unruly* 2009)

Unlocking success lies within reach—the type of reach that can be measured in views and shares. In Chapter 6 you will read about the relationship between views and shares. You will discover that the actual number of views alone does not make a social video 'viral'; rather, it is the degree to which it is shared above expectation for the level of views it has received. The Evian video falls into this category. It is an 'outlier' as it outperforms sharing expectations by more than 80 per cent given its level of views—it is truly viral.

According to our research over the last two years, getting big is largely about getting seen. To be seen by many, the distribution must be optimised—earned media alone will not result in huge reach. This may challenge the die-hard social media marketers who believe earned reach is king. Additionally, to be truly viral (where the number of shares deviate above what would be expected given the reach), a social video needs to be emotionally arousing, at least to some extent (see Chapter 3). What's more, for a video to affect sales it needs to be remembered by many people—and to be remembered the brand needs to be prominent (see Chapter 5). Finally, for an advertisement to have an impact on market share, it must reach more light buyers than heavy buyers. Chapter 8 highlights the importance of light buyers and targeting quality reach. 'Quality reach' means being distributed beyond highly targeted brand communities that skew towards heavy buyers, to a broader audience that includes buyers across the full customer base. For a social video to drive market share, targeting quality reach is vital. Evian, perhaps accidentally, ticked many of these boxes.

THIS IS NOT YOUR TYPICAL 'HOW TO GET SHARED' BOOK

This book is filled with original research from more than two years of work, five different data sets (both branded and user-generated), around 1000 social videos, nine individual studies and a large team of researchers from the Ehrenberg-Bass Institute. It reports new knowledge on how emotions are related to sharing and memory; how creative devices (such as animals) and branding prominence impact sharing; and the difference that distribution and creative variables can make. It also reveals the methods for testing arousal and discusses the use of biometrics (see the Appendix: Arousal Testing Research Method Explained).

In terms of sharing numbers, it uncovers that less contagious social videos can be winners too, even though they are low sharing. (Sound confusing? Chapter 6 will shed some light.) It also offers new findings on the mechanics of securing success. Our research illuminates that reach is still paramount and that nothing else matters if you are not seen in the first place. It challenges the usefulness of brand communities to reach the light buyers you need to increase sales.

This book suggests that, contrary to current trends, the old scientific laws still apply. It explains how existing knowledge on buyer behaviour and advertising can be applied in a world where social media rules. Marketers who have read *How Brands Grow* (Sharp 2010) will find the foundational research that underpins this new work familiar. *Viral Marketing: The Science of Sharing* builds on the science behind brands and buying. Viral success has always been a gamble, but by understanding and applying the tips in Chapter 9 you can shorten the odds of succeeding in the 'viral game of chance'.

FURTHER READING

Romaniuk, J. (2012), 'Are you ready for the next big thing? New media is dead! Long live new media!', *Journal of Advertising Research*, *52*(4), 397–99.

Sharp, B. (2010), *How Brands Grow*, South Melbourne: Oxford University Press.

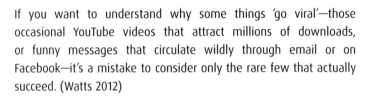

WHEN LAWS ARE NOT LAWS

KAREN NELSON-FIELD

2

If you want to understand why some things 'go viral'—those occasional YouTube videos that attract millions of downloads, or funny messages that circulate wildly through email or on Facebook—it's a mistake to consider only the rare few that actually succeed. (Watts 2012)

By explaining our research philosophy, this chapter identifies what sets this book apart from so many others on the market at the moment. In a vast ocean of generalised statements and charismatic case studies, we show just how important relevance and rigour are to good science—and just how relevant good science is to marketing.

OUR OBSESSION WITH THE SINGLE INSTANCE

At the opening address of the 2012 Advertising Research Foundation (ARF) Rethink conference in New York, Bob Barocci (then ARF President and CEO) said that in an era when advertising is changing so rapidly, marketers—and marketing researchers—are putting 'change ahead of learning'. That's certainly true in the social video space.

In medical research, the race to discovery is painstakingly slow, with years of testing, replication and repeat testing before reaching the clinical trial stage. In late 2012, Ken Kaitin, Director of the Center for the Study of Drug Development (Boston), said 'only about half of the treatments that even make it to final testing are submitted to the administration for approval ... and getting to that point takes eight-and-a-half years' (Kaitin 2012). In marketing, where research is largely unregulated, a study can be turned around in days, often with little thought as to whether the result is anything more than a fluke. The result is often a marketing 'medicine' that is far from safe and effective, yet disseminated to thousands of unsuspecting marketing managers.

Good marketing research is relevant and rigorous. Relevance cannot be achieved without rigour, but rigour can be achieved without relevance. While many marketers may think that much of the research in the social video space is relevant, in the absence of rigour it cannot be. Rigour is achieved only when the results hold again and again across different data sets, using a fully transparent process. Only when results can be generalised can they be relevant to marketing managers operating in different circumstances, markets and countries.

In statistical significance testing, the p-values are widely reported to indicate whether or not an effect is reliable and endurable. This is wrong. Such tests are merely indications of the variability in results that is introduced by using a sample to infer the behaviour or characteristics of an entire population. Geoff Cumming, a noted author in statistics reform and Emeritus Professor of Psychology at La Trobe University, states that 'researchers often use the word [significance] with a narrow statistical meaning that has nothing to do with importance' and that 'p-value gives almost no information [even] about [statistical] replication'. He shows that statistical significance can change, and change drastically, even when a random sample is drawn from the same data (Cumming 2012).[1]

---

1   To see how p-values can change even under identical conditions, see 'Dance of the p-values' by Geoff Cumming at http://tinyurl.com/danceptrial2.

More importantly, statistical significance offers no insight into the effect's ability to be applied consistently to reality; that is, whether the result will hold in another data set, from another time, in another place. The results from a single study, even if highly statistically significant, can be hideously fragile—to the point where they may be never seen again anywhere else. In 2011, when Bayer Pharmaceutical tried to replicate 67 published studies in prestigious medical journals on drug efficacy, nearly two-thirds failed to render the same result (see Prinz, Schlange & Asadullah 2011).

Often findings are ephemeral and may never be seen again anywhere else.

If this is the case in medical research, what must it be like in marketing? The only solution is to move beyond single studies. When a result holds over a range of conditions, the result can then be used predictively (see Ehrenberg & Bound 2000). It is only then that the result is of managerial significance. The research in this book has been conducted and reported on this basis:

> We believe that the main stumbling block in developing law-like relationships is that statistically minded researchers usually try to find an instant solution to a practical problem, without first investing in longer term R&D to establish what, if any, generalisable relationships exist in the data. This is like astronomers trying to predict an eclipse without having studied the motion of planets. (Ehrenberg & Bound 2000)

Replication is the key to rigorous research. Only when a result holds over a range of conditions can it be used to make predictions.

Sadly, the sprint to discovery means that successfully duplicated results are elusive. Instead, we see many one-offs, case studies and even observations claiming 'law' status. But not all laws are laws; they are typically qualitative examinations of a single instance, providing little understanding or insight for managers. This is not to say that marketers are gullible, but rather they are in the 'worship' stage of the new media adoption cycle (see Romaniuk 2012). At this stage, marketers are still so taken by the possibilities of the new platform that they only see the positives of the channel. When the wave of new devotion is so strong, it is easy to ignore research that is counter to popular commentary: 'Based on hype rather than evidence, waves of anticipatory enthusiasm put pressure on advertisers to (over) invest to avoid being left behind' (Romaniuk 2012).

Against a dangerous backdrop of trend blindness, new areas of marketing tend to grasp concepts that are less tested. It's not sexy to be sceptical of the hot new thing and no one in marketing wants to be labelled dowdy. The main danger, of course, is that marketers over-invest in the same way as the 'dot com' (boom and then bust) investors of the 1990s.

LEARNING FROM WINNERS AND FAILURES

There are always two sides to every story, so why do social video commentators only ever consider viral successes? Without studying the failures, we can't really tell what led to the success. There are currently countless social video books on the market, not to mention dozens of blogs on the topic. Most describe the characteristics of successful video and base their recommendations, rules or laws on this one-sided insight. For example:

> This book includes interviews with many people who are 'successful' in online video. (Steven Garfield, *Get Seen*, 2010)

> We'll break down the common traits of 'successful' online videos and show you how you can produce videos with those viral characteristics. (Steven Voltz and Fritz Grobe, *The Viral Video Manifesto*, 2012)

> Included in these pages [are] many new examples of 'success'. (David Meerman Scott, *The New Rules of Marketing and PR*, 2011)

> In this chapter you will learn the common traits of the 'most popular' online videos (from kids and pets to dancing and topical satire). (Kevin Nalty, *Beyond Viral*, 2010)

The research presented in this book shows that the reported common traits of success are often also common traits of failure. For example, creative devices such as animals, babies and dancing can be found in both successful and failed videos. This highlights that understanding what works isn't possible without checking out the failures, too.

> Understanding what works, without understanding what doesn't, tells only half the story and makes for poor research.

CONCLUSION

It would be nice to believe that viral success is as easy as being sneezed on. Even sensible folk want to believe that following the 'Top Ten Tips of Successful Bloggers R Us' will lead to superstardom. The reality is, of course, that social video success is more complex. Deep practical insight can only come from high-quality, reliable research, and this takes time and commitment. It is a commitment to rigour and the use of multiple data sets to ensure the results are real, generalisable and applicable that set this book apart—these, and the fact that our primary aim is to research, not to sell. This book may not have all the answers, but the answers it does have are trustworthy.

FURTHER READING

Ehrenberg, A.S.C. (1993), 'Even the social sciences have laws', *Nature*, *365*(30), 385.

Sharp, B. & Wind, J. (2009), 'Today's advertising laws: Will they survive the digital revolution?', *Journal of Advertising Research*, *49*(2), 120–6.

Wind, Y. (2008), 'A plan to invent the marketing we need today', *MIT Sloan Management Review*, *49*(4), 21–8.

3

EMOTIONS AND SHARING

KAREN NELSON-FIELD, ERICA RIEBE AND BYRON SHARP

In this chapter we investigate the creative characteristics of social videos that are shared more (and less) often. We consider how the emotions elicited by video content are related to the degree of sharing. And we shine some myth-busting light on the recipe for creative appeal.

WHAT WE KNOW ABOUT EMOTIONS AND CONTENT DIFFUSION

Much of what we know about sharing behaviour comes from research in psychology, the study of advertising and even biology. The widely accepted view is that an emotional response is important in driving further cognitive or behavioural responses. Reactions to advertising—or anything for that matter—are rarely purely rational. In particular, much advertising is of little concern to viewers and is taken in via what Robert Heath calls 'low attention processing' (Heath 2009), which tends towards emotional subconscious processing. Finally, advertising needs people to watch it in order for it to work, thus the simple emotional reaction of 'approach' rather than 'avoid' is necessary.

Recent research looking at the email sharing of 7000 articles from the *New York Times* found that 'arousal', an established construct of emotion, played an important role in driving viral diffusion (see Berger & Milkman 2012). Arousal is a physiological approach to measuring the strength of an emotional response. It is characterised by 'activation of the autonomic nervous system' or 'heightened sensory awareness' (Luminet et al. 2000). So arousal occurs during events that, for example, cause laughing or tears, take your breath away, make you sick in the stomach, make you gasp or give you goose pimples. (For interested readers, how we measured arousal is outlined in the Appendix).

While Berger was the first to use the term 'emotional arousal' in the context of online sharing, others before him had looked at how emotional strength affects the pass-along rate of a different type of content: 'memes'. Coined by the famous biologist Professor Richard Dawkins, 'meme' is a term that describes rumours, folklores, urban legends, chain letters and suchlike, all of which need to be passed along by their audience in order to survive. The idea that arousal is linked to content diffusion is also aligned to the psychology literature that refers to 'social sharing'. In this context, researchers suggest that emotional experiences are shared shortly after they occur, typically in the course of a conversation. As with memes, it is suggested that the extent of sharing is directly related to the strength of the emotion felt (see Rimé et al. 1998 and Luminet et al. 2000).

What is less agreed upon is the role that positive or negative emotions play in content sharing. The term used to describe this is 'valence'. Marketing scientists say that valence plays an important role and that positive content drives sharing (Eckler & Bolls 2011; Dobele et al. 2007; Berger & Milkman 2012). Some researchers in psychology disagree, concluding that in comparison to positive experiences, episodes of negatively valanced high-arousal emotions are equally likely to be shared (Rimé et al. 2011). Biologists, meanwhile, say that stories succeed in terms of sharing based only on their ability to evoke highly arousing negative emotions. It's a caveman thing.

So, when it comes to emotions and arousal, we consider the possibilities of high and low arousal, and positive and negative valence. There are three sizable gaps in knowledge that prompted us to consider emotions in more detail. First is the conjecture around valence—will a positive emotional response effect more video shares than a negative emotional response? Second, research to date has not examined the role of emotions in social video. Finally, and perhaps most relevant to social video marketers, previous studies have not considered the extent of sharing and its relationship with emotions. For example, psychologists have found that the number of people with whom an incident is discussed is directly related to how arousing is the emotion that is felt. Marketing researchers to date, however, have simply considered whether it was shared or not (or what was the level of claimed probability; that is, 'How likely is it that you would share this?'). This tells us little about how much more shared one piece of content is over another, relative to the emotions evoked by each video. Given that the extent of sharing is an important practical measure of viral success, we felt its absence in research presented a striking gap in our knowledge.

LET THE SEED GROW

by David Waterhouse, *Unruly*

With over 72 hours of video content being uploaded every 60 seconds to YouTube alone, brands, entertainment companies and amateur video makers offer online audiences a wealth of choice. However, this makes it tough for advertisers to ensure their video content is not lost in the crowd. If a brand merely posts a video on YouTube and expects viewers to flock to it without any kind of promotion, they are unlikely to gather many views at all.

Seeding uses paid distribution to ensure that content is visible and easily shareable on social networks, blogs, established websites, social hubs and mobile apps: in other words, native content environments, where people are already discovering, watching and sharing video content. When an advertisement is effectively seeded, it is as engaging as unbranded content. Social media users may choose to share it on their profiles, reaching even more like-minded people within the target audience.

Peer-to-peer recommendation of videos not only helps disseminate the content; it also helps to improve brand perception. When a viewer watches an advertisement that has been recommended to them by a friend, that viewer is more likely to remember the brand and see it in a more favourable light. A study, carried out by *Unruly* in association with research firm Decipher, found a 14 per cent increase in the number of people who enjoyed a video following a recommendation versus those who had discovered it by browsing. The study also found that when a viewer enjoys a video, they are 97 per cent more likely to purchase the product featured in it.

ARE YOU POSITIVELY AROUSED?

Gaps are there to be filled. Having identified apparent gaps in our knowledge of the influence that emotional reactions to social video content may have on sharing, we undertook our own research. Our findings are based upon a combination of two large data sets (n = 800 videos). Emotional reactions to each video were recorded by 28 coders (each video was examined by two coders).[1] Then, for each video, actual levels of daily sharing online were captured using aggregator websites and software. Coders were both unaware of the rates of sharing for each video and were blind to the objectives of the study.

While we understand that marketers are most interested in commercial video (that is, advertising), confining our study to just commercial videos could be misleading. Commercial videos, which we call branded videos, vary in the amount of marketing support they receive; that is, marketers conduct concurrent offline campaign activities (seeding). The degree of sharing for such videos is also likely to be influenced by the characteristics of the brand

---

1   The method for measuring emotional reaction is further detailed in the Appendix.

they are promoting, such as brand size (market share) and the category they belong to. All of these things, in addition to how 'contagious' the video is, may influence the degree to which a video is shared.

To ensure our results were 'real' and generalisable (as discussed in Chapter 2), and not due to any confounding variables, we did a separate analysis of user-generated (non-commercial) video content, as well as branded (commercial) video content. Approximately half of our videos (that is, n = 400) were branded, with the remaining videos being user-generated. Where appropriate, we show results for both types of data, or for the more appropriate half of the videos. The sample used for each result is defined throughout.

The 400 user-generated videos, along with sharing information for each video, were collected randomly from an available aggregator site (*Facediggs*). Sharing information included the number of shares per day for each video since its launch date. To allow for the valid comparison of videos that had been recently launched with those that had been available for many months, we used an average number of shares per day per video measure (total shares divided by the number of days available). The typical length of a user-generated 'campaign' that was analysed was less than 30 days, with the longest being a year. The typical length of time our branded videos had been 'on air' was much longer at around a year, with 30 per cent being over a year old. These sharing data were collected in 2011. Given that the user-generated videos were, on average, much younger (less time on air) than the branded videos, it is perhaps not surprising that they were usually less shared. What is noticeable is that both data have a very similar distribution of sharing performance, with high sharing being the exception rather than the norm.

The level of sharing in the data ranged from one share per day to just over 109,000 shares per day. As most people would expect, few videos would be classed as viral superstars, with over 50 per cent of user-generated videos achieving fewer than 500 shares per day, and only a tiny few achieving more than 10,000 shares per day (see Figure 3.1).

Figure 3.1: The distribution of video sharing performance

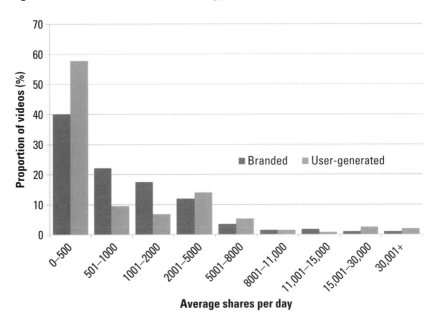

The 400 branded videos used in this study were collected randomly from UK-based agency *Unruly*, which has published the Viral Video Chart since 2006 (*Unruly* n.d.). The videos advertised a wide range of products and services, including motor vehicles, technology, fast-moving consumer goods, insurance and finance. Sharing information for each video was also collected. These data were collected in early 2012.

The level of sharing in our data ranged from three shares per day to just over 52,000 shares per day. Again, few videos could be classed as viral superstars, with 40 per cent of branded videos achieving fewer than 500 shares per day.

Table 3.1 shows that content that draws a high-arousal and positive emotional response is shared more often than content that draws any other emotional response from its audience. This is qualitatively consistent with Berger and Milkman's (2012) *New York Times* email-sharing research.

Video content that draws a high-arousal positive emotional response from its audience is shared 30 per cent more, on average, than content that draws a high-arousal negative emotional response (the next highest sharing arousal–valence group). It is shared even more in comparison to videos that draw other emotional reactions from their audiences.

Content that draws a high-arousal positive emotional response is shared more.

When we look at the combined effect of arousal (high or low) and valence (positive or negative) on average shares per day, the main effect of arousal is stronger than that of valence. This is evident in Table 3.1, which shows high-arousal (alone) videos are shared twice as often as those that draw a low-arousal emotional response (as compared with only 30 per cent more when valence is present).

Table 3.1: Average sharing for videos based on arousal and valence

Group	Total sample	User-generated	Branded
High arousal (Ha)	4446	5171	3786
Low arousal (La)	1851	2071	1625
Positive valence (P)	2948	3751	2220
Negative valence (N)	1651	1222	2172
HaP	4623	5921	3522
LaP	2203	2833	1615
HaN	3737	2652	5055
LaN	1269	959	1644
Total average	**2519**	**2832**	**2206**

Content that draws a high-arousal emotional response, regardless of valence, can be shared around twice as much as low-arousal content.

A CHARITABLE AFFAIR

Are non-profit videos different? In 2012, the viral success of the Invisible Children video on warlord Joseph Kony surprised not only the organisation but also the world, as noted by Invisible Children co-founder Danica Russell: 'We thought a few thousand people would see the film, but in less than a week, millions of people around the world saw it' (Associated Press 2012).

This campaign produced significant viral success, sparking a critical debate on the merits of the campaign. In its first 347 days online, the video had averaged more than 29,000 shares per day (typical sharing of a user-generated video is fewer than 500 per day). Later in 2012, another non-profit organisation rose to superstardom with its *Sesame Street*-style campaign. Melbourne Metro, an Australian rail authority, in conjunction with advertising agency McCann Worldgroup, redefined the typical public-service safety initiative, creating global popularity with a catchy animated video. In its first 92 days online it averaged more than 30,000 shares per day (see the box, 'Melbourne Metro goes viral').

MELBOURNE METRO GOES VIRAL

by John Robinson, Ehrenberg-Bass Institute

Melbourne Metro, in conjunction with advertising agency McCann Worldgroup, redefined the typical public-service safety initiative with a *Sesame Street*-style campaign creating global popularity (Szokan & Fazeli-Fard 2012). The three-minute video plays host to a number of cute cartoon characters dying one by one because of a variety of irresponsible behaviours. The aim was to educate young adults and teenagers to act safely around trains. These humorous yet detailed depictions of death include electrocution while getting toast out with a fork, eating a two-week-old unrefrigerated pie and selling both your kidneys on the internet. The video is accompanied by a catchy tune, in which the lyrics mirror possible causes of death, erupting in a chorus of, 'Dumb ways to die, so many dumb ways to die' ('Dumb Ways to Die' 2012). The last three scenes are the focus of the video, with the characters doing dumb things on or around railway lines, such as driving around the boom-gates and getting hit by a train, and the accompanying lyrics 'dumbest ways to die'. 'Dumb Ways to Die' was Australia's fastest spreading viral video to date, with over 27 million YouTube views in its first week; and 2,195,000 Facebook shares and 69,000 Twitter shares (*Unruly* 2012; Moses 2012). John Mescal from McCann explained: 'From the beginning we planned to make it shareable, but you can never plan for something to be the biggest viral campaign in the world' (ABC News 2012). Not only did 'Dumb Ways to Die' capture a global audience but it also created a life of its own, with an ever-growing amount of international covers and parodies such as NASA's 'Cool Things to Find'. However, the biggest factor leading to the success of the campaign was its cut-through to the teenage demographic. Mescal claimed, 'Younger people hate being told what to do, and what's really interesting about this work is it never tells you not to do it.' He went on to say, 'this demographic is hard to get to and are reluctant to share advertising but rather stories and entertainment, thus reject safety messages from authority. However this group is far more accepting when the message comes from friends, so to have teenagers singing to other teenagers about rail safety is a really gratifying thing.' 'Dumb Ways to Die' has generated over $50 million in global-earned media value at a fraction of the cost of one television advertisement, according to Mescal, and has attracted over 700 press hits, illustrating the power of viral media.

Both of these videos took very different approaches to facilitating a change in behaviour. It is likely that the many people who have seen the videos would admit to experiencing a highly arousing emotional response.

Karen Nelson-Field, Erica Riebe and Byron Sharp

However, one video would evoke negative emotions, while the other is likely to gain positive emotional responses. Both videos clearly seek to draw a strong reaction from their audiences. The enormous viral success of the Kony video leads us to question whether our findings would generalise to non-profit organisations.

To see if our finding regarding the role of emotions would generalise to charities, we gathered further information in relation to twenty videos created by non-profit organisations, such as the Animal Humane Society, British Heart Foundation, Transport Accident Commission and Greenpeace (see the 'Rethinking breast cancer' case study). We subjected this data to the same methodological and coding procedures used for our primary study of 800 videos.

Generating arousal with video content is useful for both commercial and non-profit organisations to achieve sharing success.

While the sample was comparatively small, our findings were consistent with those from the initial study. Those videos that drew a high-arousal positive emotion from their audiences were shared more often than those that drew any other emotional response. Similarly, we found a stronger effect for the level of arousal generated than for the valence of that emotional reaction. If we looked exclusively at arousal, high-arousal videos were shared around twice as often, compared to videos with low-arousal content. When we looked at both arousal and valence, content that elicited a high-arousal positive emotional response was shared around 70 per cent more on average than the next highest sharing arousal–valence group (high-arousal negative). While based on a small sample, this last finding suggests that valence, in its positive form, plays a greater role in the likelihood that a non-profit video will be shared.

RETHINKING BREAST CANCER WITH THE SUPPORT OF 'YOUR MAN'

by John Robinson, Ehrenberg-Bass Institute

In 2011, Canadian charity Rethink Breast Cancer, in conjunction with advertising agency John St., created a campaign that took the gloominess out of the breast cancer message using a fun and sexy approach (CBC News 2011). Together, they created a mobile application called 'Your Man Reminder', and used a social video to promote and generate awareness about the app. The app reminded women to perform regular self-breast examinations using TLC (touch, look and check), by receiving a pleasant automated reminder from an attractive man of their choice featured in the app (Davis 2011). With social network integration, the app allows women to share their messages and fully customise their calendars and reminders to never miss another vital breast check-up again. The charity initially developed its first video in 2011 with great success, and then created an update for the 'Your Man Reminder' by launching another sexy social video. The videos featured handsome, chiselled men explaining and demonstrating how to perform breast self-examinations and other useful information about breast health, including diet and exercise (Rethink Breast Cancer 2012). To accompany this important information, there is plenty of footage of sweaty, dreamy guys doing what men do, without their shirts on and with constant close-ups of their abs and biceps. Both videos end with actor credits, accompanied by the men dancing and showing off their god-like bodies.

The goal of the campaign was to engage women aged under 40 to promote and create awareness about the seriousness of breast health without using traditional shock advertising (*Huffington Post Canada* 2011; Davis 2011). Vice-President of marketing at Rethink, Alison Gordon, said, 'We're trying to break through all this clutter that is out there for young women and say, "Hey, this is funny and fun but really you should be breast aware." We're thinking differently about how to beat breast cancer' (CBC News 2011). Launched in 2011, the social video was immediately successful and reached two million YouTube views after going online (Company Films 2012). Not only did the video achieve a great reach online, but it also attracted media attention and appeared on many news reports all over the world (CBC News 2011). Through the use of social video, the campaign has been able to reach millions of people to create awareness about breast cancer and about the app, and encourage the younger generation of women to be breast aware.

HILARIOUS OR ASTONISHING?

There's more to high-arousal positive emotions than meets the eye. There are many different emotional reactions that can be described as being both high arousal and positive. Are some high-arousal positive emotional reactions better than others? Table 3.2 shows the 16 emotions used in the three studies.

Table 3.2: Arousal–valence emotions grid

Positive		Negative	
High arousal	**Low arousal**	**High arousal**	**Low arousal**
Hilarity	Amusement	Disgust	Discomfort
Inspiration	Calmness	Sadness	Boredom
Astonishment	Surprise	Shock	Irritation
Exhilaration	Happiness	Anger	Frustration

Table 3.3 shows the daily average number of video shares for each of these individual emotional reactions. For example, when looking at the branded data, the average number of shares for videos that elicited hilarity—a high-arousal positive emotion—was close to 2000 times per day (1929). The table shows that some high-arousal positive emotional responses are more desirable than others. For instance, for user-generated and branded videos, an exhilarating video is shared more often than one that is inspirational.

Table 3.3: Average sharing for videos drawing different emotional responses

Positive						Negative					
High arousal			Low arousal			High arousal			Low arousal		
	User-generated	Branded		User-generated	Branded		User-generated	Branded		User-generated	Branded
Hilarity	8499	1929	Amusement	2481	1377	Disgust	2700	2652	Discomfort	900	1783
Inspiration	4817	4900	Calmness	2556	1139	Sadness	322	9150	Boredom	710	985
Astonishment	1151	3946	Surprise	4209	2742	Shock	3385	774	Irritation	3389	589
Exhilaration	7972	5790	Happiness	3698	2245	Anger	7494	0	Frustration	2149	1448

Karen Nelson-Field, Erica Riebe and Byron Sharp

Looking at averages across both sets of data, videos that made audiences feel exhilaration were shared more than videos that elicited any other high-arousal positive emotion (average 6649 shares). Similarly, those that made audiences feel anger were shared more often than those that brought about any other high-arousal negative emotion.

Videos that evoke feelings of exhilaration tend to be shared more than any other high arousal positive emotion.

It is worth noting that none of the commercial videos evoked angry feelings. While some videos that elicited a high-arousal negative emotional response, such as sadness or anger, experienced reasonable levels of sharing, it is a brave brand manager who would venture into this highly provocative negative space. There is some evidence that 'norm violations' in commercial advertising, using content considered offensive and outside acceptable behaviour, will rank well against measures of attention, recall and recognition (see Dahl, Frankenberger & Manshandra 2003). However, little is known about the long-term consequences of highly provocative negative appeals on the brand.

Proceed with caution if you choose the high-arousal negative space. Little is known about its long-term consequences for the brand.

SHOULD HAVE, COULD HAVE, WOULD HAVE … DIDN'T!!

On the face of it, we can see that videos that draw high-arousal positive emotional reactions deliver a greater sharing pay-off. They seem to be more contagious. So presumably this is what expert video creators are doing: creating videos that elicit these kinds of reactions from their audiences. Right? Practitioners and academics who have been exposed to our results sometimes say these findings are obvious—that content creators already know how to create video content that will go viral. If this is indeed the case, then why do the very large majority of videos miss the mark?

Table 3.4 shows the proportion of all videos in the above-mentioned study of 800 that drew any of the sixteen emotional responses from their audiences. It appears that the most commonly produced videos are not generating the emotional responses required for high rates of sharing. What we are watching is a lot of amusement, which, even though it is a positive emotional response, is low arousal. Or worse, boredom, which is a low-arousal negative emotional response. The pattern is the same for either branded or user-generated videos, in almost identical proportions. With a reasonable expectation that creative agencies are better placed to create high-quality content, the similarity between branded and user-generated content is interesting. So while professional video creators may be aiming to create hilarious and inspiring material, they are achieving the same results as the amateurs. Both are falling well short on both hilarity and inspiration.

> While video creators may be aiming to create hilarious and inspiring material, most are falling well short on both counts.

It is perhaps unsurprising that video content that elicits a low-arousal emotional response is more common. It may be harder (and more expensive) to develop emotionally evocative material. There may also be the perception among some marketers that highly arousing content could overwhelm branding efforts, or is not brand relevant. Also, such videos are often subject to committees for approval, which tend to favour content that is least likely to either offend or excite.

Karen Nelson-Field, Erica Riebe and Byron Sharp

Table 3.4: Prevalence of emotions elicited by video content (percentage)

Positive						Negative					
High arousal			**Low arousal**			**High arousal**			**Low arousal**		
	User-generated	Branded		User-generated	Branded		User-generated	Branded		User-generated	Branded
Hilarity	9	10	Amusement	29	28	Disgust	2	2	Discomfort	3	2
Inspiration	4	5	Calmness	5	7	Sadness	2	2	Boredom	26	21
Astonishment	4	4	Surprise	3	4	Shock	1	1	Irritation	1	2
Exhilaration	1	2	Happiness	8	9	Anger	1	0	Frustration	1	1
Totals	**18**	**21**		**45**	**48**		**6**	**5**		**31**	**26**

On average, videos that elicit high-arousal emotions gain twice as much sharing as those that elicit low-arousal emotions; yet more than 70 per cent of all commercial videos evoke low-arousal emotions.

BUT 'MY' CATEGORY IS DIFFERENT

At this point, some readers may be thinking that some categories are special, and their videos are more likely to go viral. We took a closer look to see if any particular product category performed differently from the rest. The first two columns of Table 3.5 describe the proportion of all videos that drew either a high- or low-arousal response (ignoring valence) within each category. The last column shows the overall average shares per day by each category.

We can see that there is quite a bit of variation in the data. Some product categories do a better job, or have an inherent advantage over others at producing high-arousal content. But in virtually all cases more low-arousal videos are produced than high-arousal videos.

Three categories that punch above their weight in terms of the prevalence of high-arousal content are Cause/Non-Profit, Auto and Tourism. This finding is not overly surprising. Tourism and automobiles are aspirational, while much of the Non-Profit content revolves around the human spirit. Perhaps evoking aspiration and human spirit makes it easier for these categories to develop high-arousal content in a brand-relevant way. That said, as noted in Table 3.5, they still get it wrong around half of the time. For other categories, developing content that revolves around inspiration, exhilaration or (less preferably) sadness and shock may be difficult, particularly in the context of consumer switching behaviour and loyalty. Chapter 8 offers some valuable insights into how buyers behave.

A closer look at categories did, however, offer an interesting finding. Categories such as Shoes (for example, Nike, Puma), FMCG (Doritos, Coca-Cola), Retail (Walmart, IKEA) and Media Platforms (Google, Twitter) achieve higher-than-average daily sharing levels, yet they produce a lower-than-average level of high-arousal content. These categories, perhaps over all others, are particularly experienced and well funded.

Table 3.5: Prevalence by arousal group by product category and average shares per day

Product category	High arousal (%)	Low arousal (%)	Shares per day
Cause/Non-profit	50	50	1498
Auto	43	57	1921
Tourism	43	57	1074
Finance/Insurance	29	71	1512
Shoes	27	73	2606
Media platform	24	76	2880
Movies/TV programs	22	78	1466
Electronics	22	78	1751
Computer tech	20	80	1403
Mobile	19	81	2868
Gaming	18	82	2310
Retail	18	82	3747
FMCG	17	83	1881
Alcohol	15	85	1996
Fashion	14	86	1497
Fast food	8	92	960
Average	**26**	**74**	**2074**

How can a brand/category achieve more shares with fewer high-arousal videos, given that we know high-arousal shares the most? This suggests that there is more to the sharing puzzle than emotions. More is revealed in Chapter 6.

IS EMOTION A SURE BET?

Actually, no—far from it. The evidence presented in this chapter suggests that the pay-off from positive high-arousal videos is greater than for videos that generate other emotional responses. And the difference in sharing pay-off looks quite large. Yet there were also many high-arousal positive videos in our data that did not achieve much sharing success.

In fact, when we look at the ability of emotional response to 'predict' whether a video will achieve high or low sharing rates, its ability is extremely limited. Table 3.6 shows the percentage of high- and low-arousal videos that were shared more and less than the median sharing rate. Slightly more (57 per cent compared with 43 per cent) high-arousal videos shared more than the median (that is, were in the upper half). Conversely, more (52 per cent compared with 48 per cent) low-arousal videos were in the lower, less shared group. When we look at whether the emotional response was positive or negative, there is little evidence of improved predictive ability (see Table 3.7).

While these results are in the direction we might expect the predictive ability of emotions is only somewhat above chance.

Table 3.6: Arousal among higher and lower sharing branded videos

All data	High arousal (%)	Low arousal (%)
< Median sharing performance	43	52
> Median sharing performance	57	48

Table 3.7: Valence among higher and lower sharing branded videos

All data	Positive (%)	Negative (%)
< Median sharing performance	47	57
> Median sharing performance	53	43

Thus, particular emotional responses do not guarantee that a video will go viral. Yet when a video really does go viral, it is the high-arousal videos that earn massive sharing. Knowing what emotional response to go for improves your potential return, but not—it would seem—your risk. This suggests that the right sort of emotional response should be best considered a necessary, but not sufficient, condition for a video to be a viral superstar. If this is the case, as we have previously mentioned, there is more to the sharing puzzle.

Karen Nelson-Field, Erica Riebe and Byron Sharp

We address what these missing pieces might be in subsequent chapters of this book.

Focus less on creative appeal and more on emotional appeal.

CONCLUSION

We know that emotions are important. In their high-arousal form they are an important part of high-sharing video content. But in our supercharged world, funny isn't enough—only hilarious will do. Happiness is okay, but exhilarating is what we want. Negative high-arousal emotions can also prompt us to share, but which marketer is brave enough to risk offending their customers? Positive emotions are a much safer bet. Yet, while we know that evoking the extremes of emotional response makes a video more contagious, the majority of social video is still safely ho-hum. And many highly emotional videos don't go viral.

Maybe there's more to it? Continuing with the creative characteristic theme, Chapter 4 looks at creative devices. Just how do dancing, babies, animals and celebrities make a difference?

FURTHER READING

Bell, C. & Sternberg, E. (2001), 'Emotional selection in memes: The case of urban legends', *Journal of Personality and Social Psychology*, *81*, 1028–41.

Heilman, K. (1997), 'The neurobiology of emotional experience', *Journal of Neuropsychiatry and Clinical Neuroscience*, *9*, 439–48.

Poels, K. & Dewitte, S. (2006), 'How to capture the heart? Reviewing 20 years of emotion measurement in advertising', *Journal of Advertising Research*, *46*, 18–37.

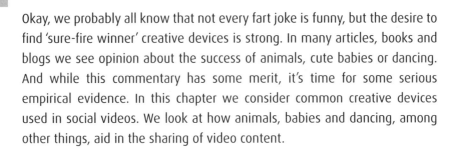

NOT ALL FART JOKES ARE FUNNY

KAREN NELSON-FIELD AND ERICA RIEBE

Okay, we probably all know that not every fart joke is funny, but the desire to find 'sure-fire winner' creative devices is strong. In many articles, books and blogs we see opinion about the success of animals, cute babies or dancing. And while this commentary has some merit, it's time for some serious empirical evidence. In this chapter we consider common creative devices used in social videos. We look at how animals, babies and dancing, among other things, aid in the sharing of video content.

THE TRUTH ABOUT CATS AND DOGS

To understand whether some creative devices are more likely to produce a desirable sharing outcome than others, we used the 800 social videos in our emotion study to identify fourteen different kinds of creative devices, and then sub-coded all of the videos.

To begin, Table 4.1 shows the average number of shares per day for each of the creative devices employed. In terms of sharing, there was wide variation between creative devices, from an average of 14,000 shares per day down to 1000 per day; however, most creative devices were very close to an average of 2000 shares per day. This variation across creative devices looks small compared with the huge variation in sharing between videos, with most achieving fewer than 500 shares per day and some achieving more than 30,000. Regression analysis showed the same thing, with each creative element typically accounting for less than 0.5 per cent of the variance in sharing. Personal triumph videos were the standout, accounting for 5 per cent of variance.

Clearly not all fart jokes are funny and sex doesn't always sell—or at least it hardly seems to encourage sharing (quite the opposite, in fact). Sadly, dancing, animals and celebrities do not appear to work any better than other creative devices at gaining higher rates of sharing.

Table 4.1: Sharing of videos using different creative devices

Creative device	Average shares per day		
	Total	High arousal	Low arousal
Personal triumph	13,925	26,672	6972
Weather/science/nature	6879	8956	5668
Baby/young child	5982	12,649	3315
Parody/comedy skit/prank	3055	5316	2374
Animal	2732	3641	2377
Dancing/singing	2279	4281	1665
Demonstration of technology	2227	2765	1904
Political/religious/community message	2134	1072	2502
Violence/comedic violence	1759	1289	1993
Celebrity	1553	1954	1409
Sport tricks/extreme sports	1398	2332	1129
Movie or game trailer	1378	1676	1252
Artistic/animation	1370	2349	1121
Sexual	1081	2264	758
Average	**2519**	**4447**	**1851**

Before you delete entire folders of dancing baby footage, there is a pattern worth noting. We reported in Chapter 3 that high-arousal content shares twice as much as low-arousal content, but videos that use babies *and* evoke a high-arousal emotion outperform this rule. The key here seems to be arousal. When a baby video evokes low-arousal emotions, it shares no more than any others with different devices. So to make real sharing gains, it is not enough to simply include a baby (or any other device for that matter). Rather, the baby in the video must produce high-arousal emotional responses from their audiences.

Babies do outperform many other creative devices, but only when the video evokes high-arousal emotions.

For other devices, content that elicits a high-arousal emotion is shared around twice as much as a video that elicits a low-arousal emotion using the same creative device.

Just in case you thought it was a matter of applying one simple rule, there are exceptions, which work in the reverse. For instance, low-arousal political/religious/community messages and violence/comedic violence videos are shared about twice as often as high-arousal videos using these same creative devices. Potentially, this is due to the niche audience segment that finds these videos relevant and appealing. For example, an anti-gun video posted to a violence-education community could end up with very high shares per day because one in five people in that community would share it, regardless of whether the content itself was arousing. If that video were to hit a mainstream audience, we might expect the level of sharing to fall in line with low-arousal rates, matching our expectation of a mass audience.

We saw one particular example of this in the videos we examined. A video that appealed for gay marriage support received high levels of sharing per day, presumably because the audience was particularly supportive of the cause. Yet it was also unanimously believed (by our multiple coders) to elicit only low-arousal emotional responses (see the 'Marriage equality: it's about time' box).

MARRIAGE EQUALITY: IT'S ABOUT TIME

by John Robinson, Ehrenberg-Bass Institute

In 2011, in an attempt to inspire change to the *Marriage Act 1961* (Cth), community advocacy organisation GetUp! created what has become the most watched gay marriage advertisement in history (Johanson 2011)—'It's Time'. The almost two-minute-long video, captured from the point of view of an unknown character, portrays the establishment and journey of a relationship with a handsome young man. The video begins with the two meeting on a boat on Sydney Harbour then moves throughout different moments they share together, such as dates, meeting the parents, moving in together and holding hands on the beach in the sun. Not only did the video portray the good times in their relationship, but it incorporated the bad as well, such as when the man's mother is critically ill and the hard time surrounding this situation. The closing scene depicts the man getting down on one knee and nervously proposing. After a brief pause the camera pans to reveal that the unknown lover is another man. Then the words 'It's time. End marriage discrimination' appear and end the video.

The campaign, which was initially designed to influence Australian voters at an Australian Labor Party conference, became a global phenomenon (Wein 2012). GetUp!'s Paul Mackay (who is one of the men in the video), said, 'We never expected celebrities would tweet about it or international sources would be interested in covering it' (*On Top* 2011). The campaign clearly demonstrated the similarities between homosexual and heterosexual relationships, with the underlying message that independent of a person's gender or sexual orientation, they should be able to spend their lives together without any barriers (Wein 2012). GetUp!'s overarching goal was to get people to watch then share the video, starting conversations about equality to create public support and further reinforce the important message (Kinser 2011). 'It's Time' not only reached marriage equality activists, but was also successful in its attempt to communicate with people who are undecided on the *Marriage Act* (Wein 2012). However, the response was not all positive, with same-sex marriage critics saying, 'You showed me a beautiful love story, then ruined it by revealing a terrible gay relationship' (On Top 2011).

WHICH CREATIVE DEVICES EVOKE HIGH-AROUSAL RESPONSES?

Do different creative devices trigger different emotional responses? Table 4.2 shows that no single creative device is more or less likely to elicit a high- or low-arousal emotional response from its audience. In fact, an equal number of videos using virtually any creative device elicited high- and low-arousal emotions. Videos employing comedy as a creative device, which are intended to be hilarious, quite clearly do not all live up to that standard. What one person thinks is funny, another may find simply lame, or even irritating.

Table 4.2: Prevalence of videos using different creative devices

Creative device	Prevalence	
	High arousal (%)	Low arousal (%)
Sport tricks/extreme sports	18	24
Parody/comedy skit/prank	12	14
Dancing/singing	13	14
Animal	10	9
Violence/comedic violence	8	6
Celebrity	7	7
Baby/young child	4	4

(Continued)

Karen Nelson-Field and Erica Riebe

Table 4.2: Prevalence of videos using different creative devices (*Continued*)

Creative device	Prevalence	
	High arousal (%)	Low arousal (%)
Demonstration of technology	5	3
Political/religious/community message	5	5
Artistic/animation	4	6
Personal triumph	3	2
Weather/science/nature	4	2
Movie or game trailer	3	2
Sexual	2	3
Average	**7**	**7**

Most creative devices have less influence than might be expected given that these devices are often the focus of industry discussion. For example, for every high-arousal video starring a baby, there are equal numbers of low-arousal baby videos. In light of these findings on prevalence, it is fascinating to look at what is most commonly used by content creators. Table 4.2 clearly shows that parodies, dancing and sports tricks are the devices of choice, even though they share no more than others.

No single creative device is more or less likely to elicit a high-arousal emotional response than a low-arousal response, or vice versa, from its audience.

A TRIUMPHANT APPEARANCE

The most successful creative approach appears to be to feature personal triumph. When a video included a creative story of personal triumph, it shared more than other creative devices. Even when it evoked a low-arousal response it did rather well. Even if it is not highly arousing, the rate of sharing far exceeds that of any other creative device. Personal triumph therefore represents the best opportunity for marketers.

Of all possible creative devices, videos that display personal triumph appear most likely to deliver sharing success.

Interestingly, despite being a more applicable creative device for ensuring sharing success, personal triumph is rarely displayed in viral video content. In our sample of 800 videos, it appeared in less than 3 per cent of all videos. This may suggest that it is difficult to do. It may also be that the few personal triumph videos were flukes.

Content creators rarely use personal triumph as a creative device.

Perhaps a safer bet are the science/weather/nature-oriented videos. These were rare, like personal triumph videos, but they also achieved very good sharing rates and, uniquely, it did not seem to matter whether they achieved high or low arousal. Nearly all of these videos achieved well above normal rates of sharing. If there is a 'sure-fire' creative approach to viral video, then this comes closest. This is a tentative but interesting finding. Interestingly, we know of no internet advertising guru who has predicted this.

SUMMARY

Across the board, the creative device used in social videos has less effect on the extent to which a video is shared than common industry discussion would suggest. For example, there are just as many unsuccessful (low-arousal and low-sharing) animal videos as there are successful ones (high-arousal and high-sharing), and just as many successful dancing videos as unsuccessful ones. The use of a particular creative device is no guarantee that a video will elicit a high-arousal emotional response, nor that it will be heavily shared. Video content, however, is generally shared more often when it is able to elicit a high-arousal emotional reaction from its audience—how it does so is perhaps of less consequence.

> The type of creative device used in video content has some impact on the degree to which such video is shared. However, there is no particular creative device that will ensure sharing success.

The best hopes that content creators have for choosing a creative device that will result in a well-shared video lies in the use of either personal triumph or science/weather/nature. Personal triumph as a creative device more often than not results in a high-arousal positive emotional response and in sharing success, but even without the high arousal it still appears to share well. Over half of all inspirational (that is, a high-arousal positive emotional response) videos exhibited this form of creative device, while 27 per cent of all shares generated by videos that drew a high-arousal positive emotional response were for videos that displayed a personal triumph. Even on the rare occasion when a video displayed personal triumph and drew a low-arousal positive emotional response, it was still shared very well.

In essence, our research on the creative qualities of heavily shared videos shows two things. First, eliciting a high-arousal (and to a lesser extent a positive) emotional response from an audience is beneficial to achieving sharing success. Second, the use of particular creative devices will not guarantee that this will occur.

CONCLUSION

It's time that dancing babies and juggling kittens stepped down off the podium and returned the keys to sharing success to the rightful owners. While we've established that identifying the rightful owners is not easy, it would be fair to say that personal triumph deserves some type of ribbon, and science/weather/nature looks perhaps to be a relatively safe bet.

We now know the roles that arousal and valence play in video sharing. We know that if viewers are to share a social video, they need to be highly aroused—exhilarated, laughing (presumably out loud) and inspired—not just smiling calmly at their screens. We know that some ways of doing this are safer bets than others, and that some offer greater potential returns, but really there are no hard-and-fast rules for the creative content of social videos.

What is most puzzling is that we know from the 800 videos in the study that videos likely to bring about the greatest sharing success are actually rarely produced. The most commonly created videos are not the type that will be heavily shared, with few content creators able to successfully execute 'personal triumph'. While it appears to be difficult to deliver these types of videos, content creators should aim to increase the emotional appeal of their videos, with less emphasis and fewer restrictions on the creative devices they use. Creators should worry less about whether the video content contains a baby, a dog or a celebrity, and instead invest in pre-testing to ensure the material makes the viewer laugh, gasp or get goose pimples.

By now you will have gained an understanding of which creative characteristics (both emotions and creative devices) aid sharing, and you will have discovered that delivering these things is rare. But this is only half of the story. In the following chapters, we investigate some of the other factors that affect the likelihood of a social video becoming a viral success.

5

BRAND PROMINENCE AND SHARING

KAREN NELSON-FIELD AND JENNI ROMANIUK

'Mirror, mirror on the wall, who's the coolest of them all?' Clearly, the answer is social video, because it's too cool to be branded. In this chapter we apply some old-school rules to the relationship between branding and sharing. Are people truly so offended by branding that it stops them from sharing a video? Previous research on brand execution elements offers us a way to test this on a sample of our video data.

DOES MY BRAND LOOK FAT IN THIS?

A common thread between schools of thought on advertising effectiveness is that for an advertisement to work the viewer needs to know the advertiser's brand. Another universally agreed principle of advertising effectiveness is that an advertisement can only affect the people it reaches. So the wider the audience, the greater is the potential impact for an advertisement. This is why there are many proponents of reach-based planning.[1] With conventional advertising, the amount of reach achieved is largely determined by budget and scheduling. With a social video campaign, the final sharing is in the hands of viewers. So social media advertisers need to create a video conducive to sharing (that is, contagious) and try to avoid anything that might hamper someone's propensity to pass it along.

This leads to the question: does the level of branding within a video put people off sharing? If your brand is noticeable, will it make people reluctant to forward it to their network? Many social video marketers think so. A 'low-profile approach' is put forward on the premise that obvious branding hampers sharing success. One brand that takes the subtle approach is Red Bull, which publicly touts its use of understated branding in videos, and connects this low-profile approach with the success of its videos in terms of viral diffusion (see the 'The art of content: Red Bull launches from space' box). Red Bull claims that brands that pepper a logo and branding over everything 'get it wrong':

> When it comes to producing video most people think about what they want to see themselves and how to get their company message across at all costs. Red Bull does the opposite. It thinks about making content that its audience will want to see and figures out how to remove as much branding as possible. (Dietrich Mateschitz, founder, Red Bull)[2]

This minimal branding sentiment is echoed in viral video 'how to' books on the market at the moment; for example, from Kevin Nalty's *Beyond Viral*: 'If you are trying to advertise via viral, dial down the marketing' (Nalty 2010).

---

1   Reach-based planning is based on evidence that shows that campaigns based on continuous reach of a broad audience are more effective for brand growth than campaigns with higher levels of frequency over a restricted audience and restricted periods of time.

2   www.brandchannel.com/home/post/2011/08/30/Red-Bull-Bullish-on-Branded-Content.aspx

THE ART OF CONTENT: RED BULL LAUNCHES FROM SPACE

by John Robinson, Ehrenberg-Bass Institute

Red Bull has been one of the most dynamic and exciting brands of the twenty-first century. The brand not only sells energy drinks but is also heavily involved in sponsoring extreme sports and events such as the 'Red Bull Stratos'—a space-diving stunt by Austrian Felix Baumgartner in 2012. Its energy drinks have great physical availability—consumers can now buy their products from every corner of the world—but the brand has also become a video-publishing empire (O'Brien 2012). Red Bull's advertising is uniquely different from other brands in terms of content and product placement. Rather than placing a full-page advertisement in a magazine or running a television campaign focusing on the product or its taste, Red Bull predominately uses content marketing to provide consumers with extreme and extraordinary video, which in return associates the brand with positive attributes and engages viewers (O'Brien 2012). In its content campaigns, Red Bull doesn't use overt branding tactics to directly promote its products but rather uses BMXs, snowboarders, skateboarders and motocross riders to promote the brand itself. Instead of having frequent scenes featuring Red Bull's distinct can, the content contains extreme scenes of snowboarders scraping the snow off the top of trees and back-flipping off walls, and BMX riders grinding rails—with just the occasional glimpse of the Red Bull logo. These videos don't contain close-up shots of the Red Bull brand or product, but these images are visible, whether it be on bike jumps or athletes' clothing. Red Bull 'de-emphasise what they place on the brand and its products and emphasis on creating interesting and visually compelling content' (Rick 2012). Founder of Red Bull, Dietrich Mateschitz, said, 'It's an efficiency product. I'm talking about improving endurance, concentration, reaction time, speed, vigilance and emotional status. Taste is of no importance whatsoever' (Shayon 2011). This belief is reflected in Red Bull's online campaigns, with the company producing amazing content that their audience wants to see while minimising their branding effort (Shayon 2011). In 2007, the company developed Red Bull Media House, which has been responsible for creating, filming and distributing extreme content around the world, and which Mateschitz believes has been the most important line extension Red Bull has invested in (Shayon 2011).

A recent television study, using a combination of eye-tracking technology and data on zapping behaviour (channel switching), showed that the degree of brand prominence[3] had a negative effect on the decision to view a commercial (see Teixeira, Wedel & Pieters 2010). More recently, the same authors claimed that these results are possibly transferable to social videos. They suggested that prominent branding may have an effect on video diffusion as it can cause viewers to stop watching and consequently not share the video (Teixeira 2012). However, this is speculative and the authors provided no evidence to back up their claim.

The key argument put forward to suggest that prominent branding can cause more harm than good relies on the potential negative relationship between creative quality, as judged by the viewer, and level of branding. However, empirical evidence in this space is largely in favour of either no relationship or a positive relationship between advertising likeability and correct branding levels (Kennedy et al. 2000). Testing of the execution elements of branding has shown no relationship between the amount of branding and the viewer's liking of the advertisement. Branding execution elements can be described as how many times it is shown visually, or spoken, and how early it appears in the advertisement (see Romaniuk & Hartnett 2010).

Care and discretion is required when interpreting eye tracking or other biometric research used for testing when the brand appears. A drop in biometric readings can easily be misinterpreted; it may not be a negative reflection on the brand, but rather a reflection of the difference in our processing of familiar versus novel stimuli. When faced with familiar stimuli, such as the brand, the brain can relax, as a familiar stimulus is easy

---

3   The authors define prominence as a combination of branding execution tactics such as visual frequency, size relative to the screen and duration.

to process. In contrast, when faced with novel stimuli, such as the rest of the advertisement, the brain needs to remain active. (We talk more about biometric testing in the Appendix.)

So to prompt a mind to think of your brand more often, each exposure needs to work hard for the brand that is advertising. It needs to be prominent, clear and directly linked to the brand. Taking a subtle approach to branding makes it harder for your customers to know who is advertising. We question the value of any marketing communication that is intentionally poorly branded. If clear branding turns out to diminish the likelihood of a video being shared, then the very value of social video as a marketing tool should be questioned.

Using poorly branded advertising is like throwing away your marketing budget.

HOW MUCH BRANDING IS TOO MUCH?

How a brand is executed influences the viewers' likelihood of noticing the brand. In 2009, in the *Journal of Advertising Research*, Romaniuk described the combined findings of all studies over the past two decades that had tested objective measures of branding execution[4] and correct brand recall (Romaniuk 2009). The findings delivered three key tactics for increasing brand prominence:

- *Reveal the brand early*—this gives the brand a chance among those people who mentally or physically switch off from the advertising.
- *Show it visually at least four times in 30 seconds*—this makes the brand a more dynamic part of the advertisement and so more likely to attract viewer attention.
- *Say it verbally at least once*—this is to reach those who do not have eyes on the screen, but are still listening to the advertisement.

Knowing that branding prominence is positively linked to advertising recall, we decided to test whether the 'low-profile approach' to brand execution gives a video a sharing advantage. We did this by sub-coding 200

---

4   Objective measures of branding execution included branding frequency, duration and entry timing.

of the 400 branded videos in our existing data from Chapter 3. We sub-coded them by brand execution factors that are evidenced to contribute to the prominence of the brand within an advertisement, or have been put forward as important branding execution elements. These brand execution factors are (Romaniuk 2009):

- *visual frequency*—how many times the brand is seen in the video
- *verbal frequency*—how many times the brand is heard in the video
- *first brand entry timing*—the time that elapses before the brand is present
- *cumulative brand duration*—the amount of time the brand is present throughout the total duration of the video.

The sample of 200 videos was selected to fully represent the total population of 800 videos in terms of the number in each arousal–valence group. We also ensured there was variation in the data in terms of branding levels (high and low), sharing numbers (high and low), video duration (long and short) and product categories.

EVIDENCE THAT VIDEOS TYPICALLY TAKE A LOW-PROFILE BRANDING APPROACH

We begin by describing the averages of all measures coded (see Table 5.1). There is clear evidence that social videos tend to take a low-profile approach to branding. The brand is present on average for only 20 per cent of a video. The frequency distribution is J-shaped, with 44 per cent of videos having 10 per cent or less branding (see Figure 5.1).

Table 5.1: Brand execution factors (averages)

Measure	Average
Video length	89 seconds
Early branding	
Time until first brand entry	32 seconds
Percentage time until first brand entry	38%
Percentage of videos with branding in the first 10 seconds	46%

Measure	Average
Visual frequency	
Number of times the brand is shown visually	5
Average seconds per visual frequency	1 per 18 seconds
Verbal frequency	
Number of times the brand is spoken	0.8
Percentage of videos that say the brand once	32%
Duration of branding	
Cumulative brand duration	16 seconds
Percentage of brand duration to total video length	20%

Figure 5.1: Percentage distribution of brand duration in videos (n = 200)

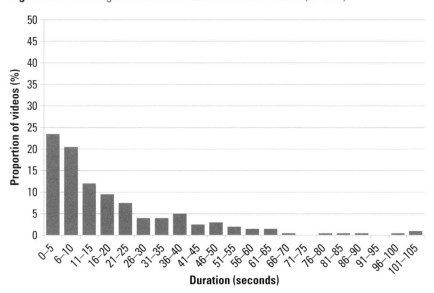

Based on prior evidence of what helps the brand be noticed, we see two findings that concern us. The first is that the branding is rarely present early in the video. On average, the brand doesn't even enter the video frame until one-third of the way through. So for most videos to have any effect, the viewer must watch the first one-third. This is a long time to keep someone's attention on the internet. Given that the average video in our study lasted 89 seconds, this means that the viewer's attention must be kept for a minimum of 30 seconds. Bear in mind that 30 seconds is the average length of most television commercials.

For social video success, it is important to remember that there are two behaviours you want from the viewer. The first is that the initial viewer recognises and knows the brand, so you can influence their future propensity to buy the brand. By not branding the video early, you miss those who watch a few seconds but decide not to continue. Some studies suggest as many as 90 per cent of a video's audience watch only the first 10 seconds, then switch off (TubeMogul, cited in Carlson 2008). Only 46 per cent of our videos revealed the brand in the first 10 seconds, which means 54 per cent might miss any branding opportunities for 90 per cent of their audience.

> On average more than a third of a social video elapses before the brand is revealed.

The second finding relates to visual frequency. Our videos averaged 89 seconds in length, which is about three times that of the average television commercial; however, on average, the brand was only visually present five times. This is a visual brand presence once every 18 seconds. Hold your breath for 18 seconds. That's a long time between branding, isn't it? Given the amount of engaging activity that occurs within a video, it is easy to see how the brand might be missed.

> On average, social videos have the brand present every 18 seconds.

ARE VIDEOS DIFFERENT?

Before we looked at the relationship between branding and sharing, we decided to compare these descriptive findings to other media types to see:

- whether other media types delay branding entry
- whether the level of branding overall is similar.

Table 5.2 consolidates previous knowledge of branding execution practice in television and online commercials and combines it with our new knowledge of social videos. As well as describing the results for the full sample, we isolated all videos that were around 30 seconds in length so that we could directly compare the absolute numbers of branding to television commercials.

We can see in Table 5.2 that videos are well under-branded compared to television commercials. Social video marketers expose the viewer to the brand (visually and verbally) around 30 per cent less in the same 30-second time frame and for 30 per cent less duration (total seconds present). The table also highlights more explicitly the concern with entry timing noted in the last section. It shows that only 37 per cent of all videos have any branding presence in the first third. This figure is sobering compared with the 59 per cent for television and the huge 73 per cent for online advertising.

Table 5.2: Current brand execution practice across media

Measure	All videos (n = 200)	Videos (28–33 seconds) (n = 38)	Television (30 seconds) (n = 1500)	Online video ads (5–30 seconds) (n = 100)
Total frequency (average number shown and heard)	6	4	6	2
Visual frequency (average number shown)	5	2	4	2
Verbal frequency (average number heard)	1	2	2	0
Early presence (percentage where brand in first third)	37	32	59	73
Dual mode (percentage with brand executed in both modes)	6	4	90	4
Cumulative duration (average seconds present)	16	7	10	13

Source: Adapted from Romaniuk (2009).

Social videos display a lower level of branding than television commercials and expose the viewer to the brand around one-third of the number of times in the same time frame.

Of further concern is the proportion of social videos where the brand was executed in both verbal and visual mode. We know that a verbal mention combined with a visual cue can help to encode information more thoroughly, giving the brand a better chance of being noticed and remembered (Romaniuk 2009). Our data revealed that only 6 per cent of all social video branding occurs in dual (verbal and visual) mode, compared with 90 per cent on television.

Only 6 per cent of all branding in a social video occurs in dual (verbal and visual) mode, compared with 90 per cent on television.

THE BRANDING AND SHARING RELATIONSHIP

The results from the previous section show clearly that creators of social video typically take a low-profile approach to branding. But is this really necessary? Given the lack of rigorous research around branding and sharing, we decided to test this ourselves.

Our variable of interest was the average shares per day. We tested whether each of the individual brand execution elements were linked to lower sharing of videos. We then looked at the combined results, where the three brand execution tactics are summed together to create a scale. The scale ranges from 0 (no effective tactics present) to 3 (all three effective tactics present).

Table 5.3: Comparison of brand execution of videos by sharing

Average sharing per day category	Percentage until first brand presence	Visual frequency	Percentage of videos (1+ verbal)*	Percentage duration	Combined execution
Lowest quartile	34	3.8	36	22	1.3
Second quartile	44	6.2	36	22	1.1
Third quartile	34	3.8	34	19	1.3
Highest quartile	39	5.5	24	18	1.1
Total averages	**37**	**4.8**	**33**	**20**	**1.2**

*Percentage of videos (1+ verbal) = the proportion of videos with a minimum of one verbal brand mention.

Our findings show that regardless of when the brand becomes present, and how often and how long the brand is present, the level of sharing does not significantly vary. Even when we combine the tactics, the highest quartile of sharing does not differ from the lowest sharing quartile.

No relationship is evident between how much sharing a video achieves and the level of branding executed.

IT WAS OVER BEFORE IT STARTED

Previous chapters show a clear relationship between high-arousal emotions and social video sharing. Past research into advertising has failed to find a relationship between the level of brand execution and the appeal of an advertisement. So we wondered—perhaps there is no relationship between the amount of branding and the level of arousal–valence of a social video.

Table 5.4 demonstrates why branding does not have a negative effect on sharing. As you can see, the high-arousal positive videos experience more shares than any other arousal–valence group. This high-sharing group also displays more branding than other groups, and significantly more for dual visual and verbal modes. The level of branding does not dilute high-arousal positive emotions.

High-arousal positive videos display more branding than the other groups, yet still share the most.

Table 5.4: Brand frequency and arousal–valence groups (n = 200)

	Average shares per day	Total frequency (shown and heard)*	Visual frequency (shown)	Verbal frequency (heard)	Cumulative duration (seconds present)
High arousal positive	4509	8.3	7.0	1.30	101
Low arousal positive	1072	4.7	4.0	0.69	79
High arousal negative	2051	4.5	4.4	0.11	132
Low arousal negative	1193	5.3	4.6	0.64	91
Total averages	**1868**	**5.6**	**4.8**	**0.79**	**89**

*$p = {<}0.05$

The level of branding present has no effect on the degree to which a video will arouse viewers.

It is important to note that we are not claiming that higher levels of branding are driving the higher arousal positive scores. The evidence to date is more in favour of no relationship at all. Our findings show that the brand's presence does not hamper the capacity for emotion-inducing creative. Therefore, there is no excuse to not brand your videos. Further, the similarity of results between social video and television advertising suggests that we can use the body of knowledge about effective television execution techniques and apply them to videos.

APPLYING AGE-OLD BRAND RULES IN THE NEW WORLD

There is consistent evidence that some brand execution elements increase the chance of the viewer noticing and processing the brand name (Romaniuk 2009). The brand name should be:

- *used early*—get the brand in early to capture those who might switch off physically or mentally
- *visually frequent*—make the brand a dynamic, noticeable part of the advertisement
- *spoken at least once*—ensure you capture those who have visually switched off but are paying attention to the sound

It is important, however, to remember that branding execution is the means, not the end. These criteria help in that they provide an objective framework for you to assess the quality of the branding of any marketing activity. The endgame for brand execution is to ensure that every viewer of the video knows which brand that video is from. These guidelines are like the basic ingredients for a cake. Ideally, they need to be included, but you still have a lot of discretion over the type of cake you are baking. At the end of it all, how you brand is less important than making sure the brand is a noticeable, attention-grabbing part of the video.

CONCLUSION

Contrary to popular belief, the brand is not the enemy. It will not single-handedly destroy your bid for excellence in viral videos. There are so many other ways you can do that!

We found no evidence that an obvious brand presence hampers sharing, nor that it restricts your ability to achieve high-arousal positive emotional responses. The popular notion of the need for a low-profile approach is a myth. Far greater danger exists in not branding well, particularly if the video achieves a large audience of people who don't share and don't notice the brand. Any efforts spent on video exposure will be wasted.

While some people like to think that television is a second-rate player in today's brave new world, the similarity in results for both media reminds us that we shouldn't throw out the old rule book just yet. Past research into television advertising brand execution—to understand what makes the brand a noticeable part of any video—is still applicable, whether it is for an advertisement or a viral video. Brand execution guidelines still have a lot to tell us about the ultimate usefulness of our viral success.

6

REACH [STILL] REIGNS

KAREN NELSON-FIELD, ERICA RIEBE AND BYRON SHARP

> Rather than trying to create the next 'viral hit'—the strategic equivalent of throwing a Hail Mary pass—a lot of marketers have stopped crossing their fingers and started optimizing their content so that millions of people will discover, watch, and [then] share it. (Jarboe 2013)

> You have to have great shareable content ... You [also] have to have paid advertising. (Jim Farley, CMO of Ford)

We now know what sort of emotional reaction to aim for when creating our (hopefully viral) video, and that this emotional reaction will increase the sharing potential and slightly enhance the chance that the video does go viral. We also know the sort of creative approach or device that is slightly more likely to go viral. In total, however, we are a long way from a perfect viral recipe. And in terms of stating what creative approach to take, this is possibly about as far as we'll ever be able to go. So what else can we do to enhance views?

In this chapter, we examine other factors that determine how often a social video will be shared and, ultimately, viewed. Sharing absolutely depends on viewing; videos effectively have to be viewed before they can be shared. But sharing also drives viewing. More viewing means more sharing, and more sharing means more viewing—and because of this two-way causality we see a strong relationship between views and shares. We document this relationship and use it to discuss how videos become successful.

AVAILABILITY

Irrespective of creative content, the role of video availability must, on average, have a considerable effect on the viral success of video material. In this chapter, we draw an analogy between viral videos and consumer brands. First, consumer brands must fulfil a consumer need—this has usually been confirmed through consumer and market testing prior to launch. Second, to grow (or even maintain market share) a typical consumer brand needs availability, both mental and physical (Sharp 2010). Mental availability is the propensity for a brand to be thought of in buying situations (Romaniuk & Sharp 2004). It is built over time and maintained with ongoing advertising that is well branded, stands out in clutter and reinforces memory cues that help its accessibility at buying moments. Physical availability (or distribution) is also usually necessary for brand growth, meaning that the brand is easy to buy. If a brand is physically but not mentally available, it risks not being seen on shelf. Every major packaged-goods company has plenty of case histories of good-quality new brands that have gained wonderful distribution, due to the company's large sales force, but failed to move off the shelf.

We can draw an analogy between the availability required for brand growth and the availability required for a video to become a viral superstar. While it's common for viral video commentators to place more emphasis on perfecting the creative aspects of content rather than on determining how that content can be most broadly distributed, it is almost assumed that great content will drive lots of sharing, and thus viewing, which in turn will drive even more sharing, and thus viewing. Even if this is true, in the real world, social video success could be more the result of amazing levels of seeded viewing, due to publicity and advertising in other media (which content creators can simply pay for). Even a social video that achieved only modest sharing might achieve a great many views if it started with a large seeded audience.

FEW VIEWERS SHARE

Duncan Watts, principal researcher at Microsoft and author of *Six Degrees: The Science of a Connected Age* (Watts 2004), does not have a romantic view of how to create viral video success. He says there is 'no free lunch' and that the likelihood of a video spreading to millions from a small seed is negligible. Furthermore, on the rare occasion where this does happen, it is virtually impossible to repeat such success—like winning the lottery twice.

His argument is based on the notion that only a fraction of those who view video content share it—even for the most shared videos. He describes rate with which views are converted to shares as 'the reproduction rate', which he considers to be a measure of how contagious the video is. In a 2007 paper, *Viral Marketing for the Real World*, Watts presented his case on the concept of 'big seed marketing' using real-world examples (Watts, Peretti & Frumin 2007). The concept is based on the realistic notion that the large majority of videos are not superstars and therefore will have a reproduction rate that is lower than 1 (where 1 means that every person who views it shares it with another person; that is, 1:1). Viral growth is a function of both time and this rate of reproduction. Over time, every video naturally burns out, and how long this takes is a function of its reproduction rate. The closer the reproduction rate is to 1, the slower the rate of decay (see Table 6.1).

The concept of 'big seeding' suggests that investing in a large base limits risks associated with viral marketing. Even if the video is of average quality (in terms of its ability to generate sharing), when a campaign starts with a larger pool of seeds, the gains in absolute earned reach will outweigh the associated costs. The gains in possible views are larger, and they also can be

Table 6.1: Example of Watts's 'big seed' concept

Degree of separation from initial view	Every fourth person shares once (R = 0.2) Initial paid views		Each second person shares once (R = 0.5) Initial paid views		Four people out of five viewers share it once (R = 0.8) Initial paid views	
	100,000	1000	100,000	1000	100,000	1000
2	20,000	200	50,000	500	80,000	800
3	4000	40	25,000	250	64,000	640
4	800	8	12,500	125	51,200	512
5	160	2	6250	63	40,960	410
6	32	0	3125	31	32,768	328
7	6	0	1563	16	26,214	262
8	1	0	781	8	20,972	210
9	0	0	391	4	16,777	168
10	0	0	195	2	13,422	134
11	0	0	98	1	10,737	107
12	0	0	49	0	8590	86
13	0	0	24	0	6872	69
14	0	0	12	0	5498	55
15	0	0	6	0	4398	44
16	0	0	3	0	3518	35
17	0	0	2	0	2815	28
18	0	0	1	0	2252	23
Total views	**125,000**	**1250**	**199,999**	**2000**	**490,993**	**4910**
Incremental views (earned reach)	**25,000**	**250**	**99,999**	**1000**	**390,993**	**3910**

achieved over a far shorter period than if the initial seed is smaller. Table 6.1 demonstrates this in the row that describes the incremental views relative to the initial seed and reproduction rate. Even for a video that shares really well (the R = 0.8 columns on the far right), there are far more earned views when the brand starts with a large seeded audience. Logically, when a video is initially viewed by relatively few people, it cannot possibly be shared all that much.

A video that is viewed by relatively few people cannot be shared by many.

Of course, it is also theoretically possible for a video to have a high sharing rate due to the average viewer passing it on to several (even many) people. Even so, they have a lot of non-sharers to make up for and some shares fall flat by reaching people who have already seen the video and so are less likely to view it again—and certainly less likely to share it again. Real viruses (diseases) fade out this way when they start hitting people who already have the disease or have had it and so are immune. Many people's social networks have very high overlap—that is, your friends are your friends' friends—so their capacity to share to people outside of your friend network is constrained. This doesn't mean that a video can't go from a small base of original viewers to a very large base due to sharing. Videos can 'go viral', but logic suggests that it might be exceptionally rare and that seeding might be well worthwhile in enhancing the total views, even for video that is particularly shareable.

Watts's logic suggests that viral videos will benefit most from being helped along. But enough of this theorising—let's look at the relationship between viewing and sharing. Figures 6.1 and 6.2 show the relationship between viewers and sharers in the video data we have discussed in earlier chapters of this book. The figures demonstrate the similarity in this relationship across both sets of data (that is, both branded and user-generated videos). As expected, we see that these metrics are strongly related—the more a video is viewed, the more it will be shared; and the more people who share it, the more it is viewed.

Figure 6.1: Relationship between viewers and sharers—branded

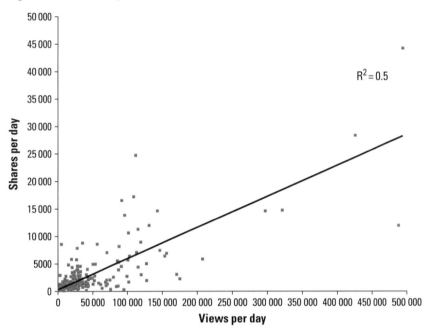

Figure 6.2: Relationship between viewers and sharers—user-generated

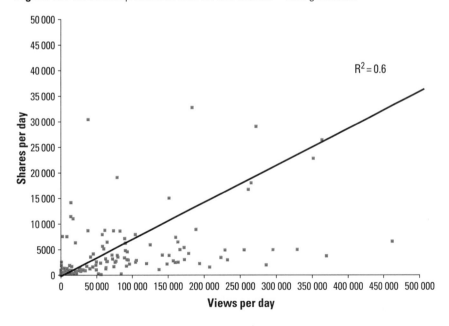

What is really interesting is how few viewers share. There are more than ten times as many people who view a particular video on a day than share it. Put another way, this means that more than 90 per cent of viewers don't share. And we'd expect those that do to mostly share with only a few people; only a very tiny fraction of sharers (and an infinitesimal fraction of total viewers) share with a large number of people. All of this suggests that 'virality' tends to get you only so far, and that even a very contagious video is still very risky, as the spread could easily sputter out, like a bushfire when the wind turns it back onto ground that it has already burnt:

> The reason is simply that when influence is spread via some contagious process, the outcome depends far more on the overall structure of the network than the properties of the individuals who trigger it. Just as the forest fires require a conspiracy of wind, temperature, low humidity, and combustible fuel to rage out of control over large tracts of land, social epidemics require just the right conditions to be satisfied by the network of influence. (Watts 2012)

More than 90 per cent of viewers don't share.

AMPLIFY YOUR WORLD

by Cat Jones, *Unruly*

The probability that a video will be shared once it has been viewed depends on the context in which that view takes place. *Unruly*'s analysis shows that the share rate (shares per view) of a given video varies with both the discovery mechanism of the viewer and the existing level of engagement of a wider audience with the video. Viewers discovering the video through a trusted recommendation are more likely to share it than viewers who arrive at the video by browsing, and viewers who view the video knowing that it is getting popular are more likely to share it than viewers who do not.

Sharing amplification effect #1: personal recommendations

Having collected sharing data on over 329 billion video streams, *Unruly* has found that someone viewing a video on the recommendation of a person they trust is much more likely to go on to share it than someone who simply stumbles across the video online. For example, a viewer who watches a video posted on Facebook by a friend whose video postings she usually enjoys is fairly likely to click 'like' following the view. The 'like' publishes the video to her timeline, sharing it with her friends in turn. Across the 2500+ campaigns that we have run, we can see that views that result from personal recommendations tend to have a much higher share rate than views that do not, sometimes up to an order of magnitude higher. A certain proportion of viewers discovering a video while browsing will go on to share it—let's say 2 per cent—but that 2 per cent share rate could be amplified to as much as 20 per cent for the views that result from those initial shares.

Sharing amplification effect #2: popularity

If high levels of viewing and sharing occur in a short period of time, the increasing popularity of the video can act to amplify the share rate even further. People like to be part of the latest, newest video trend that everyone is talking about, and this is particularly true of trend-spotters, who tend to share content more than mainstream viewers. This means that a viewer who knows that a video is getting popular (for example, if they've seen it trending on Reddit) is more likely to share it than a viewer that doesn't—but only while it's new, before it hits the mainstream and becomes old news. Hennig-Thurau et al. (2012) found that the effect of popularity on engagement (including sharing) peaks in the first three to seven days of a video's life.

CREATING CONTAGIOUS VIDEO

We use the term 'contagious' to describe social videos that have a high propensity to be shared among those that view it. Some diseases are much more contagious (easy to pass on) than others, but that doesn't mean they will necessarily spread more—timing could be wrong (for example, seasonal changes) or people might take precautions to stop infection.

We wanted to identify those videos that were more contagious than others, and so had more potential to spread. The relationship we observe between views and shares allows us to set expectations for sharing performance of videos, so we can identify when a video is doing particularly well (or particularly poorly) at sharing, given how many people are viewing it. It is rare that a video is able to produce far more shares than we would expect it to given the size of its audience (that is, its views). While rare, however, there are some exceptions that test this rule and it is the characteristics of these more contagious videos that content creators are most likely to be interested in. Just as we find a few rare superstar performers, we also see a few real duds. In either case, we can learn a great deal from these exceptions to the rule that shares are largely correlated with viewing levels.

So what makes one video more contagious than another? What characteristics are indicative of a video that defies the odds and is shared more than we would expect? Equally, are there some defining characteristics of a video that is destined for failure? Obviously this is again where creative quality plays a role.

To understand this we investigated the creative characteristics of those videos that were shared 75 per cent more (and less) than we would expect given their views (see Figure 6.3). Remember that this does not mean that these outliers are all big (highly viewed and shared) videos; social videos with low views can perform above expectation, but they are still small (which is why distribution is so important). This is where much of the research on social video goes wrong. For the most part, big videos are big because they are well distributed, so looking at the creative characteristics of only these big videos tells us nothing of their differences over poorly performing videos. In fact, those big videos could even be poorly performing on sharing, given their large number of views. This may be why we find that some creative aspects of videos—and advertising more generally—can be equally present in videos that are deemed to have been successful and unsuccessful. Perhaps this is because our definition of 'success' is wrong.

Less contagious videos can be winners, too (if they are well seeded or supported); it's all in the interpretation of success.

Karen Nelson-Field, Erica Riebe and Byron Sharp

Figure 6.3: Outliers (branded): 75 per cent above or below expected share performance

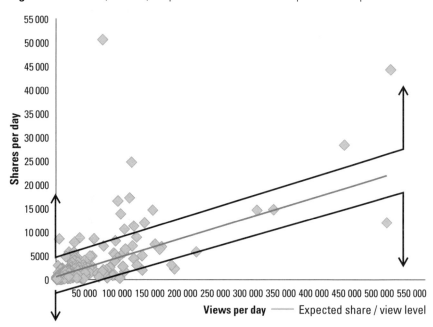

Rather than defining success by the total views that a video has been able to achieve, we now define it by the extent to which the video deviates from this expected relationship between shares and views. In essence, this embodies the real meaning of viral success; that is, outstripping the level of performance that was simply bought through seeding efforts.

Where these superstar videos differ from the large majority is in the creative execution they deliver. For example, for videos that perform at the expected rate of sharing given their views, a tiny proportion of that share performance is accounted for by the emotional response elicited by the creative quality of the video (because most videos in the sample generate low-arousal emotional responses). But when we separate the outliers from the rest of the sample, first we can see that there is a significantly greater proportion of outliers that evoke high-arousal emotions by comparison to non-outliers (see Table 6.2). Second, when drilling down into the sharing performance of these superstar performers, we see that a huge 90 per cent of the sharing can be explained by the fact that they are able to elicit high-arousal positive emotions from their audience by using personal triumph as a creative device. This is why these creative elements were consistently present in videos that generated high levels of shares per day (see Chapter 3).

Table 6.2: Percentage high/low arousal among outliers and non-outliers

All data	Outliers (%)	Non-outliers (%)
High arousal	**60**	25
Low arousal	40	**75**

Of course, a brand in a category like toilet tissue or ready-made sauce may find it difficult to deliver video creative that is exhilarating, inspiring and triumphant. For these types of brands, however, all is not lost. In Chapter 7, we discuss why generating any high-arousal emotion is of great value for a social video campaign in terms of other success metrics.

> Videos that are shared more than we would expect given the size of their audience evoke high-arousal emotions (such as exhilaration) and exhibit creative that involves personal triumph.

Interestingly, when a video underperforms against expectations, a whopping 90 per cent of its performance is the result of views. That is, they have nothing else that makes a contribution to the extent to which they are shared. No emotions had a significant effect on their poor performance. Thus video content needs to be widely viewed in order to simply gain an average amount of sharing. Performing any better than this (and really excelling in relation to shares) requires the generation of high-arousal inducing content.

CONCLUSION

A virtuoso playing a violin in her bathroom may be fabulous but cannot be widely appreciated. Aiming to create highly contagious video is a very worthy objective, but the evidence is strong that there is still great benefit in seeding

Karen Nelson-Field, Erica Riebe and Byron Sharp

and supporting that video; that is, buying views that will then result in more shares and more views.

The reality is that most videos aren't particularly contagious, so this recommendation to buy views, to ensure wide availability, carries even more weight. The creative characteristics are still important, but a waste if the video isn't seen. Getting your video viewed by a wide audience will at least make it easier to also deliver good sharing metrics.

If we take a definition of viral success more narrowly to mean purely how contagious it is (how likely it is to be shared by a viewer) then the winners have some defining characteristics—notably their ability to elicit high-arousal emotional responses from their audience, typically through displaying personal triumph. But plenty of contagious, positive high-arousal videos still hardly get any shares, and hardly any views.

Most marketers are interested in total views—sharing is just a means to an end—and even highly contagious videos can still sputter out. So we return to Watts's theory of big seeding. You can have a very contagious video, but if you start with a small base, the total views will typically be small. Of the 400 branded videos investigated here, fewer than 10 ticked both boxes: high viewing and higher than expected sharing. So it seems superstars are very rare indeed. This adds more weight to the notion that investing in a larger base limits risks associated with viral marketing.

Be careful not to underinvest in distribution or over-invest in creative.

FURTHER READING

Romaniuk, J. & Sharp, B. (2004), 'Conceptualizing and measuring brand salience', *Marketing Theory*, 4:4, 327–42.

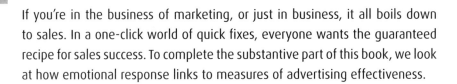

7

THE PAY-OFF

KAREN NELSON-FIELD WITH JENNIFER TAYLOR AND NICOLE HARTNETT

If you're in the business of marketing, or just in business, it all boils down to sales. In a one-click world of quick fixes, everyone wants the guaranteed recipe for sales success. To complete the substantive part of this book, we look at how emotional response links to measures of advertising effectiveness.

EMOTIONS AND MEMORY

While developers of video strive to get seen, it is equally as important to be remembered. Why? Because advertising works by refreshing and building memory structures that are linked to the brand (Sharp 2010). Most of a brand's consumers are light buyers, who also buy from the competitors. They rarely give any brand much thinking time. Even frequently bought brands aren't bought as frequently as you might think, so it's easy to forget which brands we buy. Advertising reminds you that you once bought the brand and offer a gentle nudge to buy it again. Memory cues make it easier for the brand to be thought of and noticed at the critical time of purchase. So, logically, an advertisement must be remembered on some level to make an impact at the point of purchase.

> Advertising reminds that you once bought the brand—and gently nudges you to buy it again.

Advertising needs two critical elements to nudge memories: being well branded and getting noticed. Being well branded is about making it easier for customers to recognise that *you* are doing the advertising and not your competitor (we discussed the importance of branding and its effect in Chapter 5), while advertising can only succeed if it gains (and holds) the attention of its viewer. Getting noticed requires content that can cut through the clutter in order to hold the viewer's attention. Consumers care little for advertising at the best of times, but when a platform is highly cluttered the chance of the advertising cutting through the clutter diminishes.

> Advertising needs two critical elements to be remembered: being well branded and getting noticed.

Advertising clutter is said to affect people in a number of ways. These include:

- reducing the brain's capacity to absorb and make sense of messages where competing stimuli are present (overload and interference theory; see Malhotra, Jain & Lagakos 1982; May, Hasher & Kane 1999).
- forcing us to only provide attention to stimuli that is deemed relevant (selective attention theory; see Seamon 1980).
- triggering avoidance behaviours due to our natural resistance to forced advertising volume (reactance theory; see Brehm & Brehm 1981).

Clutter, and its negative effect on memory, has been found to generalise in the context of radio, television, magazines and newer media such as Facebook. With around 100 hours of video uploaded to YouTube each minute, the social video space is no different. So what makes content cut through the clutter, get noticed and aid memory? It would be easy to think that a high number of views and being recalled go hand in hand. People often assume that popularity aids memory, but it doesn't. Our data show that highly viewed videos can also be poorly recalled and vice versa.

In Chapter 3 we discussed the role emotions play in the sharing success of video. We know that video content that evokes high arousal and positive emotions is shared the most. We know that 'more likeable' ads tend to be more immune to clutter (Hammer, Riebe & Kennedy 2009) and that likeability can be linked to emotional campaigns (Wood 2012). Could arousal (our measure of quality content) be linked to better recall? Can arousal assist in the quest to cut through, get remembered and generate sales?

Keeping in mind that for research findings to be reliable and useful they must be generalised across varying conditions, we used two data sets to explore the link between emotions, recall and sales: the user-generated sample (400 videos) as described in Chapter 3, and a second set of branded data for the purpose of this analysis.[1] All coders were asked to recall which videos they remembered seeing one week after exposure (user-generated data) and two weeks after exposure (branded data). We did this by asking them to describe briefly the content of a video they remembered coding. For example: 'The one where the man was walking his dog, then he found himself transformed into another world full of chocolate bars.' The descriptions were cross-referenced with each data set. We then matched recall with the individual coders' emotional response. This ensured the emotion experienced by the individual coder was directly related to the video being remembered. While we acknowledge that advertising recall does have its faults, grounded mainly in the unreliable nature of memory, overall recall is still a universally accepted measure of advertising effectiveness.

To allow for the fact that each coder was presented with three times the number of low-arousal videos as high-arousal videos (user-generated data only), we considered recall as a proportion to the total sample within each arousal group, rather than as a proportion to the total videos recalled. In other words, of all the high-arousal videos presented, what proportion of

---

1   We collected forty additional commercial videos (courtesy of *Unruly*) and had them coded using the identical coding framework, as discussed in the Appendix. These videos were first launched at either the 2011 or 2012 Super Bowl.

them were recalled? (Rather than: of all videos recalled, what proportion were high-arousal?) Looking at the data this way ensures we are describing the recall of each arousal group, not its prevalence in the sample. Tables 7.1 and 7.2 describe the results for each data set.

Table 7.1: Recall by arousal group (user-generated sample)

Arousal group	Sample size (original data)	Number recalled	Percentage of total sample
High arousal (Ha)	99	29	29
Low arousal (La)	301	28	9
Positive (P)	255	41	28
Negative (N)	146	16	11
HaP	76	21	28
LaP	179	20	11
HaN	23	8	35
LaN	123	8	7
Sample number	400	57	

Table 7.2: Recall by arousal group (branded sample)

Arousal group	Sample size (original data)	Number recalled	Percentage of total sample
High arousal (Ha)	23	16	70
Low arousal (La)	17	3	18
Positive valence (P)	37	18	49
Negative valence (N)	3	1	33
HaP	22	16	73
LaP	15	2	13
HaN	1	0	0
LaN	2	1	50
Sample number	40	19	

The data shows that highly arousing content is linked to better recall. We find that social videos that evoke high-arousal emotions, in both positive and negative form, are the most remembered. In fact, they are remembered around three times more than videos of low arousing content. This is consistent across both sets of data.

Videos that elicit high-arousal emotions cut through the clutter and are remembered the most.

While we know that high-arousal positive videos share the most, we can see that high-arousal negative videos are remembered slightly more than high-arousal positive videos in the user-generated data. That said, when we ignore arousal, videos of positive valence are remembered more overall. This is consistent with the sharing results. Note that this finding relates only to the larger user-generated sample. Not surprisingly, very few creators of Super Bowl ads incorporated negative emotions.

What is interesting here is that valence, when combined with the effect of arousal, seems to play slightly less of a role in memory than it does in sharing. Even though they remember them, viewers are less likely to share high-arousal negative videos. This suggests that why someone shares might be the last little piece of the sharing puzzle. Motivation lies outside marketer control and, consequently, sits outside of the scope of this research. Literature linking critical motivation factors, particularly altruism, to sharing (see Ho & Dempsey 2010) offers some insight into this part of the puzzle.

The knowledge that high-arousal negative videos are remembered is consistent with research on 'norm violations'. Norm violation describes advertising that is considered offensive and outside acceptable behaviour. Such content is said to rank well against measures of attention, recall and recognition (Dahl, Frankenberger & Manshandra 2003). However, creative content incorporating anger, shock, sadness and brand relevance would be extraordinarily difficult to compose. Among other things, the content would run the risk of being poorly branded. The level of risk increases when we consider how little the industry knows about the long-term consequences of norm violations on the brand. A campaign that evokes high arousal and negative emotions would be ill-advised.

> Arousal is about getting some additional reach, but it is also about being remembered. Views alone can't do this.

At the individual emotion level, exhilaration is most successful. Overall, 65 per cent of all exhilarating videos in both samples were recalled. Hilarity rates a very close second, with 51 per cent. In the negative valence group, content that makes you angry cuts through the most, with 60 per cent of such videos being recalled (keeping in mind that there are no anger-evoking videos in the Super Bowl data).

> The most commonly recalled positive emotion is exhilaration.

The lesson here for marketers is that creative decisions are just as important as media placement decisions. Regardless of how many views an advertisement achieves, if it is poorly remembered it is ineffective. If you needed any more convincing about brand prominence after Chapter 5, it is worth remembering that even if your creative can be recalled and it has a high level of views, your advertisement is still ineffective if the brand is misattributed to your competitor. Ouch! So while your highly arousing video content will be shared and cut through the clutter, it's critical that the brand be prominent and easy to identify.

EMOTIONS AND SALES

Over the past decade or so the collective discoveries relating to how people buy and how people watch advertising, and advances in neuroscience's understanding of how the brain works have shifted the paradigm of how advertising works and its impact on sales. We now know that as shoppers we are habitual with split loyalties, as viewers we are inattentive and distracted, and our memory isn't as good as we thought it was. The old view, which was focused on an informative, consciously persuasive model, has shifted to a low-involvement, non-rational and emotional one. Because we don't have a perfect memory, and we switch between the small number of brands in our favourite group, we need to be reminded of the brands on offer. Memory is a key piece in this puzzle.

We have discussed how high-arousal emotions dually focus our selective attention and aid memory. But what does this mean for sales? Sales are the reason why brand advertising exists. Marketers spend billions of dollars to both protect and grow revenue. Metrics such as views, shares, recall and other 'hot' metrics such as 'engagement' are intermediary to the ultimate goal—sales.

The general notion of emotions in advertising is that they are a prominent driver of brand favourability, even when rational content (that is, the offer) has no effect. It is this brand favourability that is considered an important moderator in rather effortless and non-rational purchase decisions (Heath 2009). To date, one of the most commonly collected metrics associated with emotions is advertising 'likeability'. The promise of likeability was made apparent by the seminal ARF Copy Research Validity Project, where likeability was the single best predictor of sales-effective copy given branded pairs (a sales 'winner' and a sales 'loser') of commercials (see Haley & Baldinger 1991). Since that time, metrics have now developed beyond self-report responses to physiological measures. In a similar vein to the ARF project, Wood (2012) recently published results of BrainJuicer's FaceTrace™, a facial detection measure spanning seven core emotions. Results suggest that their 'Emotion-Into-Action' score was a superior predictor of IPA Effectiveness Award winners compared with other common pre-testing metrics; for example, persuasion, cut-through, brand linkage and message comprehension. While on the surface this seems a win for those who endeavour to link emotions and sales, the dependent variable remains an in direct measure of real sales effects.

Today advertising pre-testing companies, using more complex yet conveniently obscure testing methods, are fiercely promoting emotion measurement as the means to determine the potential of short-term sales success. While we are not disputing the robustly researched role that emotion plays in advertising, we do question any reported effect of emotions on sales from marketing-mix modelling. This approach is flawed when measuring advertising effects among other activities. Marketing-mix modelling, and similar methods, is based on aggregate time series data and relies on the ability to pull apart the effects of the various components of, for example, advertising versus promotion. It is difficult to disentangle and is often inaccurate as there can be interactions between elements of the marketing mix. Additionally, we know that aggregate sales don't always reflect competing upwards and downwards sales movements. Something may act to boost sales (like advertising) at the same time something is acting to suppress sales (such as a downturn in the economy). Further, much advertising is intended to protect share, yet without variation in sales, market-mix models cannot estimate the relationships between marketing variables.

The widely accepted gold standard for measuring advertising effects is single-source data. Single-source data captures individual household brand purchases and their exposure to brand advertising. Rather than requiring increases and decreases in sales overall, single-source data can see changes in the households that did and didn't receive the advertising. Single-source data is difficult to collect and to date has been particularly cost-prohibitive, which is why pre-testing agencies do not use it (Jones 1995).

Single-source data is the gold standard for measuring advertising effects.

At the Ehrenberg-Bass Institute we work with some of the world's leading corporations. For more than a decade, big brands like Coca-Cola, Unilever, Procter & Gamble, Turner Broadcasting and many others have supported our work to uncover new knowledge about marketing through our R&D program (see www.marketingscience.info). For us, this means access to data that can span decades, countries and categories, to study the impact of emotions in advertising on a household's propensity to buy a brand.

THE SINGLE-SOURCE EXPERIMENT

We are currently using single-source data and our established emotions framework to examine the relationship between emotions evoked by content and actual in-market sales.

To ensure consistency across studies we are applying the same methodology to coding emotions as we had to all previous sets of data in this research. Our experiment aims to extend our previous work by considering how the same emotional responses are linked to an alternative measure of success: sales. In particular, we are testing whether:

1 commercials that evoke high-arousal emotions are positively related with a higher level of sales than commercials that evoke low-arousal emotions

2 commercials that evoke positively valanced emotions are positively related with a higher level of sales than ads that evoke negatively valanced emotions

3 commercials that evoke high arousal (and) positively valanced emotions are positively related with a higher level of sales than ads that evoke low arousal (and) negatively valanced emotions.

If you are on the edge of your seat to read the results here, unfortunately, like an end of season cliffhanger, this may leave you asking 'but who shot JR?' At this point we are unable to describe the study in any more detail, other than to tell you work is underway, in collaboration with think-tanks within industry, and that our results will be published by year's end.[2] You may be asking, 'Well, what was the point of this section, then?' If we can better understand the mechanisms by which emotion leads to a real behavioural response to advertising, we can be much more efficient in our campaign execution. However, it's important to understand that the only way to achieve this is through single-source data. This takes time and we wanted to tell you that we are well and truly in the race.

---

2   If you would like to be notified of the outcome of this study or wish to have your single-source data tested, please contact either Nicole Hartnett or myself at the Ehrenberg-Bass Institute.

So be wary of 'quick fix' studies that will suggest this has already been solved. Studies that tell you that purchase intent, brand attitude or engagement are as good as sales are wrong. Only data that has a direct link to individual-level sales can be used to describe real sales effects.

CONCLUSION

While many marketers work dutifully on ways to appeal to the market, what they really should be doing is working their way into the corners of the mind—of many minds. We know that memory is vital in the link between advertising and sales. We know that highly arousing content does stand out and is remembered more. Our research agenda is now looking for a direct link between highly arousing content and sales.

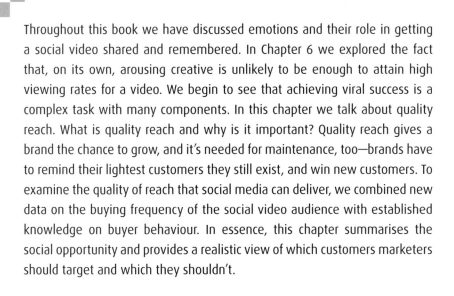

8

THE SOCIAL OPPORTUNITY

KAREN NELSON-FIELD WITH KELLIE NEWSTEAD

Throughout this book we have discussed emotions and their role in getting a social video shared and remembered. In Chapter 6 we explored the fact that, on its own, arousing creative is unlikely to be enough to attain high viewing rates for a video. We begin to see that achieving viral success is a complex task with many components. In this chapter we talk about quality reach. What is quality reach and why is it important? Quality reach gives a brand the chance to grow, and it's needed for maintenance, too—brands have to remind their lightest customers they still exist, and win new customers. To examine the quality of reach that social media can deliver, we combined new data on the buying frequency of the social video audience with established knowledge on buyer behaviour. In essence, this chapter summarises the social opportunity and provides a realistic view of which customers marketers should target and which they shouldn't.

Reach is important, but it needs to be quality reach to achieve maintenance and growth.

HITTING THE RIGHT TARGET

Targeting strategies that spend time and money focusing on reaching heavy or most loyal brand buyers have long dominated marketing thinking. This thinking is superficially logical—waste fewer dollars on those who are less profitable and spend more on those who love the brand and buy more. This infatuation with heavy buyers stems from two sources:

1 the unreasonable notion that consumers care greatly about brands—this is seen in, or perhaps due to, 'engagement' hype driven largely by those who stand to profit from the idea

2 the mythical Pareto Law—this is a marketing 'rule of thumb', theorising that 80 per cent of sales come from just 20 per cent of buyers (heavy buyers).

That heavy buyers are the more appealing targets is largely undone by our knowledge of how consumers actually behave: how they buy and how they respond to advertising. These next few sections explain buyer behaviour and advertising response. By the end of the chapter, you will understand how this relates to social video.

CONSUMERS ARE NOT THE MARRYING KIND

Marketers are enamoured with the idea of exclusively faithful consumers. The ideals of 'brand love and brand passion' are invariably the goal for most marketers, typically facilitated through social media 'engagement' and one-to-one interaction. Marketers try to turn every consumer into a Don Gorske. A Wisconsin resident and McDonald's loyalist, Mr Gorske reportedly eats, on average, 14 Big Macs per week; he has only ever gone a few days without eating a Big Mac (*Guinness Book of Records* 2013). In his 40-year love affair with McDonald's, it is reported that he has eaten more Big Macs than anyone else in the world and amassed a vast collection of McDonald's merchandise (Gillie 2013). Mr Gorske is a model consumer for McDonald's; he is faithful beyond reason—and most stomachs. He is also highly unusual. Most consumers freely and unforgivingly cheat on one brand with another.

Brands simply have to accept that switching is commonplace. Unlike the self-confessed obsessive-compulsive Gorske, most consumers prefer a little variety in their lives. 'Little' is the keyword; they want variety but they don't want to work too hard for it. It would be fair to say that consumers are unfaithful, lazy and not really marriage material.

The vast majority of a consumer's purchasing is habitual and dictated by subconscious processing, particularly in repeat-purchase markets. Considerable data demonstrates that we have steady buying propensities (Sharp et al. 2012). We buy from brands we are well acquainted with and we fulfil our category requirements from an established group of brands (brand repertoire). Within this established group there is usually one more frequently purchased brand (the main partner); then there are other brands on the side that are purchased less often. This is because the brands in our repertoires are largely substitutable—they all wash our clothes, quench our thirst, take us from A to B, etc. (Ehrenberg, Uncles & Goodhardt 2004).

It is easy for a brand to be forgotten. For marketers, the goal of advertising is staying within the brand repertoire and trying to break into a new one. Consumers will switch easily to a competing brand in their repertoire when one is not available or when another is on price promotion that particular week. In essence consumers are faithful to a lucky few. This polygamous loyalty is a far cry from the monogamous relationship marketers would hope for, or for which they are falsely encouraged to aim.

So what does this have to do with social video? Firstly, video sharing is not driven by brand love. In his book *Beyond Viral* (2010), Kevin Nalty says, 'The cat on a skateboard is more interesting than your brand'—and he is right (not that we are saying a video should be poorly branded). Second, while the Pareto Law is a widely applied 'rule of thumb', it is misleading. It is actually the light buyers who are the most valuable for brand growth. One study suggests that the top 20 per cent of a brand's buyers (the heavy buyers) on average contribute to about 50 per cent of sales (Sharp & Romaniuk 2007), not 80 per cent, as previously accepted. Further, the brand's lightest 80 per cent of customers are not only important for maintenance and growth, but also contribute to half of today's sales, and more of tomorrow's.

LIGHT BUYERS MATTER

A brand's customer base is accurately described by a negative binomial distribution (NBD). The NBD describes the frequency distribution of purchase rates across a population of consumers for a single brand or category. For most brands, this means a customer base made up of a high proportion of light buyers (shoppers who have a low to close-to-zero purchasing rate), fewer medium buyers and very few heavy buyers (see Sharp 2010, chap. 4).

However, there is more to the 'light buyers matter' story. What the NBD tells us is that as a brand grows it achieves higher market penetration and higher average purchase rates, but the shape of the distribution *always* stays the same. Figures 8.1 and 8.2 show a typical buying distribution. Because the shape of the distribution is constant, the bulk of change is seen among the brand's very many light buyers and non-buyers. Light buyers contribute to the bulk of brand growth. Those who are already heavy buyers of the brand are unable to give any more of their category buying; there is no room to gain extra sales from them. Light buyers have plenty of scope to buy again.

Figure 8.1: Percentage of Coke buyers buying Coke X times

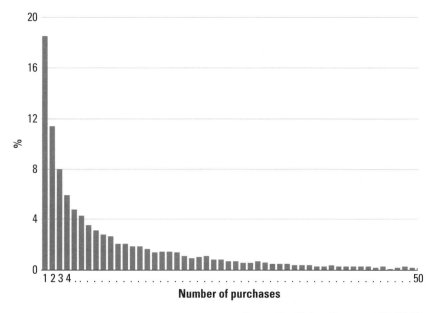

Source: The Nielsen Company, USA (2007).

Figure 8.2: Percentage of Kellogg's Special K buyers buying Kellogg's Special K X times

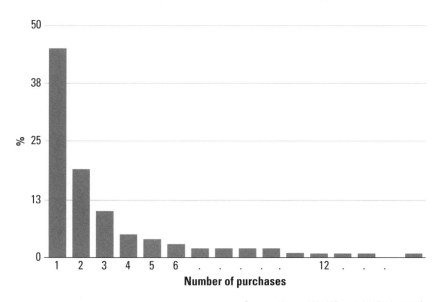

Source: Kantar WorldPanel, UK (July 2007).

The widespread fit of the NBD ultimately provides the basis for understanding the significant role that light buyers play in growing a brand. To grow in size, a brand needs to increase the size of the consumer base. To do this, advertising (and social videos) must reach large numbers of light buyers. This is what we mean by quality reach.

Gaining many more buyers is key to brand growth, even though most of them buy infrequently.

CAN BRAND COMMUNITIES GIVE YOU THE REACH YOU NEED?

Given many social videos are launched around brand communities, we wanted to test the reach a typical brand community would attract. We chose to test this in a Facebook brand community. The analysis uses two data sources. First, we collected self-reported purchase data from Facebook fans of two (unnamed) brands from two different repeat-purchase categories— chocolate and soft drinks. Second, we used actual consumer panel data for the *same* brands for direct comparison. For both sets of data, we classified these purchase categories into non-buyers (not bought in the three months), light buyers (bought once), moderate buyers (bought two to three times) and heavy buyers (bought four or more times).

Figures 8.3 and 8.5 illustrate actual panel data that shows the typical NBD pattern is evident, as expected. There are many non-buyers and light buyers, and far fewer heavy buyers of the brand. Figures 8.4 and 8.6 show that the fan base delivered by Facebook is skewed towards the heaviest of the brand's buyers, demonstrating that it is completely opposite to the expected pattern (see Nelson-Field, Riebe & Sharp 2012 for full details).

Figure 8.3: Buying concentration across the whole customer base for a chocolate brand

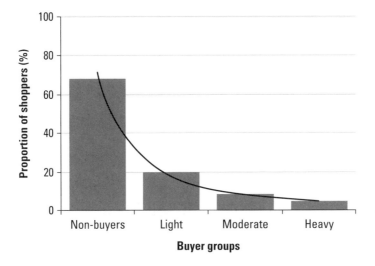

Figure 8.4: Buying concentration across the Facebook brand fan base for the same chocolate brand

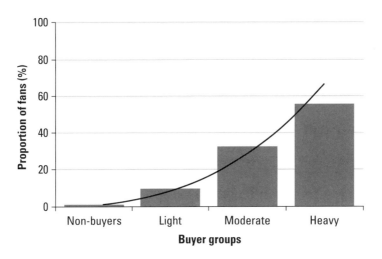

Figure 8.5: Buying concentration across the whole customer base for a soft drink brand

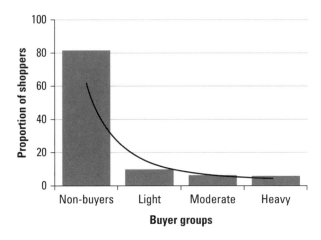

Figure 8.6: Buying concentration across the Facebook brand fan base for the same soft drink brand

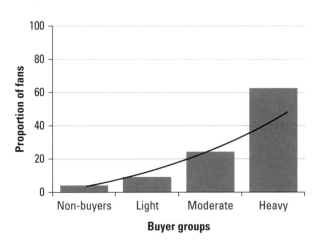

A third study, also undertaken at the Ehrenberg-Bass Institute, has applied the same methodology, but with television viewers. Figure 8.7 shows the buying concentration of the 2012 Super Bowl audience for the same soft drink brand. The television findings are more consistent with a typical population of a brand's buyers—it skews to the lighter buyers of the brand.

Figure 8.7: Buying concentration of the 2012 Super Bowl viewing audience for the same soft drink brand

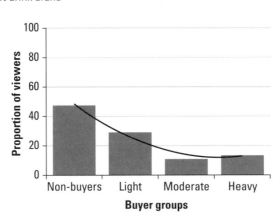

So, in looking at three groups of buyers—Facebook fans self-reported purchase, consumer panel data and Super Bowl television audience—we can demonstrate that Facebook fan pages are inefficient at providing vast reach to light buyers when compared with television; that is, Facebook fan pages are not reaching the most fundamental customers needed for brand growth. If you are wondering whether it's just a Facebook thing, the results were the same for a separate study conducted on the Twitter platform, also undertaken at the Ehrenberg-Bass Institute.

These findings are also consistent with a recent study that considered reach across media types (Romaniuk, Beal & Uncles 2013). Romaniuk's research confirmed that the audiences reached by mass media (such as television and outdoor) do skew to the light brand user, while niche media (such as word of mouth and social media) skew to the heavier brand user. Brand communities are where heavy buyers live. Given what we know about the importance of light buyers for brand growth, the thinking behind targeting brand communities, which contain large numbers of heavy buyers, is flawed. It is a false economy to think that these communities are more efficient targeting options.

Facebook fan pages are inefficient at providing vast reach to customers that are most fundamental for brand growth.

So what does all this mean for social video? How should videos be distributed if not within targeted communities? The answer is to treat the distribution of social video as a television campaign—pay for quality reach. Many idealists will cringe at this blasphemous suggestion that destroys the Utopian possibility of money for nothing. Chapter 6 provided the background for this approach, when we discussed how much sharing is driven by views. The following research consolidates the argument.

ARE YOU LOOKING AT ME? WHO SEES VIRAL VIDEO?

We chose to test two of the top twenty most viewed social videos of all time. These were highly seen videos which had never been aired on commercial television. They had an average of 14 per cent penetration rate among the US population, which is on par with the top-rating television program *NCIS,* on CBS (13.7 per cent).[1] To keep things consistent, we chose one video from each of the same categories as the previous research (soft drink and chocolate) and applied the same methodology. We also separated the panel into those who are Facebook fans of each brand and those who are not. We did this to ensure that we had a sample that had not seen the video as a direct result of being a brand fan.

---

1   Source: Nielsen, Primetime Broadcast Programs, United States, week of 28 January 2013. Viewing estimates on this page include live viewing and DVR playback on the same day, defined as 3am to 3am. Ratings are the percentage of TV homes in the US tuned into television.

Our findings reveal that viewership, outside of a Facebook brand community, reaches more broadly across the customer base. Figure 8.8 shows the results for the chocolate category. The buying concentration of those who have seen the video but are *not* Facebook brand fans is NBD distributed. That is, distribution is skewed more to non- and light buyers of the brand.

By direct comparison Figure 8.9 shows the purchase distribution of video viewers who *are* fans of the brand. The distribution again skews towards heavy buyers and is more aligned to what we would expect of a niche brand community.

Viewership, outside of a Facebook brand community, provides more useful reach, in terms of brand growth.

Figure 8.8: Buying concentration of those who have seen the video outside of the brand community—chocolate brand

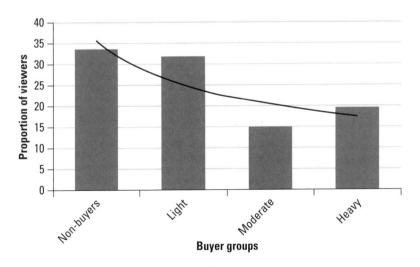

Figure 8.9: Buying concentration of those who have seen the video and are Facebook fans—same chocolate brand

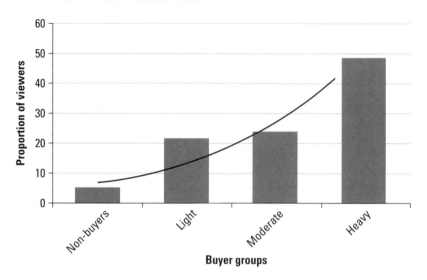

While we acknowledge that we can't be certain that participants who did claim to be fans of the brand actually saw the video as a direct result of being in the brand community (that is, saw it on the brand page due to being a fan), the shape is markedly opposed to those who didn't. We are comfortable that for the large majority at least, this would be the case. It is what we would expect in a brand community. Table 8.1 summarises the reach findings discussed so far. It illustrates clearly the consistency across studies and across categories.

The main implication is that some media skew towards light buyers, and that this media is particularly valuable. In this case, we can see that social video viewership via Facebook brand communities skews towards heavy buyers. It is not as effective at reaching light buyers when compared with a more broadly distributed video.

Table 8.1: Percentage buying concentration of all data analysed

	SOFT DRINK				CHOCOLATE			
	Super Bowl (n = 397)	Social video (non-fans) (n = 206)	Facebook (n = 520)	Social video (fans) (n = 202)	Super Bowl (n = 397)	Social video (non-fans) (n = 220)	Facebook (n = 1000)	Social video (fans) (n = 171)
Non-buyers	47	28	4	3	28	34	1	5
Light	29	7	9	3	34	32	10	22
Moderate	11	14	24	10	23	15	33	24
Heavy	13	13	63	13	15	20	56	49

CONCLUSION

When it comes to growing a brand, we've known for some time that light customers hold the most promise. And now we know where to find them. They're not your Facebook friend or your Twitter follower. They're everywhere else—presumably watching television or just randomly searching the web looking for an opportunity to cheat on their favourite brand.

The serious side of this finding is that marketers who need to be careful with their budgets will have to reframe how they invest their marketing dollars. They should be wary of over-investing in the relatively small numbers of already heavy buyers who typically congregate around online brand communities. Rather, they should be investing in strategies to reach the valuable light buyers.

FURTHER READING

Heath, R. & Fieldwick, P. (2008), 'Fifty years using the wrong model of advertising', *International Journal of Market Research, 50* (1), 29–59.

Newstead, K., Taylor, J., Kennedy, R. & Sharp, B. (2009), 'The long-term sales effects of advertising: Lessons from single source', *Journal of Advertising Research, 49* (2), 207–10.

9

LAST DRINKS

KAREN NELSON-FIELD

NOT THE SAME, BUT NOT THAT DIFFERENT

So, are we talking black with white stripes or white with black stripes? The answer lies in your marketing background. If you sit in Camp Persuasion, you would be feeling the unsettling tremors of marketing structures shifting beneath you. If you sit in Camp Science, the ground feels steady in the knowledge that many old rules still apply even though the media landscape has changed.

There is no denying that social media marketing has sparked a chasm of difference in the marketing profession, with age and technical capacity often chosen as weapons on the battleground. But it all starts with our initial assumption of how brands grow and how advertising actually works. Those who work from the principles of marketing 'text' believe that advertising works through persuasion and message comprehension. This means 'teaching', mostly already heavy buyers, using a message that extols the brand's benefits to viewers until they conform. Buyer conformity will then lead to continued brand love and increased loyalty. If you work from the principles of marketing science, you will understand that advertising works largely by refreshing, and sometimes building, memory structures by evoking an emotional response. We buy from a small repertoire of brands so advertising should reach large numbers of lighter buyers, refreshing mental availability.

Advertising via shared video still works the same way. Sure, the way video content is distributed is vastly different, but how consumers respond to advertising remains steadfast. People are responding to social media in the same way they have responded to radio, television and the internet. In this book we have shown that a social video is most successful—in terms of shares and recall—when it can cut through the clutter with highly emotive content. This is no different from traditional advertising. The obvious difference lies with content distribution and the ability to gain earned reach using the newer media platforms. As with all new things, the hype around the potential of social media is disproportionate to reality. Gambling for such reach with creative content alone doesn't always pay off. Most videos don't go viral.

This research shows that while quality creative is important, the easy solution for getting 'big' in the social video space is to pay to kick-start the campaign. When more people view it, more people share it—simple. This is not all that dissimilar to the nature of applause. Researchers have found that the quality of a performance does little to drive the amount of applause an audience gives (Mann et al 2013). Instead, the research shows, the total number of other audience members already 'infected' by clapping influences an individuals' probability of joining in. So applause causes applause, as does reach cause reach. While 'rent-a-crowd' seems an unlikely option for a performer who wishes to 'optimise' success, buying reach is an easy option for social video marketers.

Now, if you are thinking that the cost of seeding defeats the purpose of cost-effective viral campaigns, then wake up. There is no free ride in business, and no one will be giving you a free ticket to quality reach.

RESEARCH INSIGHTS SUMMARY

Here is a summary of key findings and insights in this book. For more information, visit www.marketingscience.info or www.karennelsonfield.com.

ON THE RESEARCH PHILOSOPHY (CHAPTER 2)

- Often findings are ephemeral and may never be seen again anywhere else.
- Replication is the key to rigorous research. Only when a result holds over a range of conditions can it be used to make predictions.
- Understanding what works, without understanding what doesn't, tells only half the story and makes for poor research.

ON EMOTIONS AND SHARING (CHAPTER 3)

- Content that draws a high-arousal positive emotional response is shared more.
- Content that draws a high-arousal emotional response, regardless of valence, can be shared around twice as much as low-arousal content.
- Generating arousal with video content is useful for both commercial and non-profit organisations to achieve sharing success.
- Videos that evoke feelings of exhilaration tend to be shared more than any other high arousal positive emotion.
- Proceed with caution if you choose the high-arousal negative space. Little is known about its long-term consequences for the brand.
- While video creators may be aiming to create hilarious and inspiring material, most are falling well short on both counts.
- On average, videos that elicit high-arousal emotions gain twice as much sharing as those that elicit low-arousal emotions; yet more than 70 per cent of all commercial videos evoke low-arousal emotions.
- Focus less on creative appeal and more on emotional appeal.

ON CREATIVE DEVICES AND SHARING (CHAPTER 4)

- Babies do outperform many other creative devices, but only when the video evokes high-arousal emotions.

- No single creative device is more or less likely to elicit a high- or low-arousal emotional response from its audience.
- Of all possible creative devices, videos that display personal triumph appear most likely to deliver sharing success.
- Content creators rarely use personal triumph as a creative device.
- The type of creative device used in video content has some impact on the degree to which such video is shared. However, there is no particular creative device that will ensure sharing success.

ON BRAND PROMINENCE AND SHARING (CHAPTER 5)

- Using poorly branded advertising is like throwing away your marketing budget.
- On average more than a third of a social video elapses before the brand is revealed.
- On average, social videos have the brand present every 18 seconds.
- Social videos display a lower level of branding than television commercials and expose the viewer to the brand around one-third of the number of times in the same time frame.
- Only 6 per cent of all branding in a social video occurs in dual (verbal and visual) mode, compared with 90 per cent on television.
- No relationship is evident between how much sharing a video achieves and the level of branding executed.
- High-arousal positive videos display more branding than the other groups, yet still share the most.
- The level of branding present has no effect on the degree to which a video will arouse viewers.

ON VIEWS AND SHARING (CHAPTER 6)

- A video that is viewed by relatively few people cannot be shared by many.
- More than 90 per cent of viewers don't share.

- Less contagious videos can be winners, too (if they are well seeded or supported); it's all in the interpretation of success.
- Videos that are shared more than we would expect given the size of their audience evoke high-arousal emotions (such as exhilaration) and exhibit creative that involves personal triumph.
- Be careful not to under invest in distribution or over-invest in creative.

ON EMOTIONS, MEMORY AND SALES (CHAPTER 7)

- Advertising reminds you that you once bought the brand—and gently nudges you to buy it again.
- Advertising needs two critical elements to be remembered: being well branded and getting noticed.
- Videos that elicit high-arousal emotions cut through the clutter and are remembered the most.
- Arousal is about getting some additional reach, but it is also about being remembered. Views alone can't do this.
- The most commonly recalled positive emotion is exhilaration.
- Single-source data is the gold standard for measuring advertising effects.

ON REACH QUALITY AND TARGETING (CHAPTER 8)

- Reach is important, but it needs to be quality reach to achieve maintenance and growth.
- Gaining many more buyers is key to brand growth, even though most of them buy infrequently.
- Facebook fan pages are inefficient at providing vast reach to customers that are most fundamental for brand growth.
- Viewership, outside of a Facebook brand community, has more useful reach outside of the customer base, in terms of brand growth.

ON AROUSAL TESTING METHODS (APPENDIX)

- To limit confusion when testing, pairs are useful when the underlying scale of measurement is subjective.
- When coding emotions, using multiple coders can minimise subjectivity.
- A well-constructed coding system that displays high inter-coder reliability *and* can predict the level of subsequent video sharing is 'measurement gold'.

FURTHER READING

Ehrenberg, A.S.C. (1988), *Repeat-Buying: Facts, Theory and Applications*, London: Oxford University Press.

Jones, J.P. (1997), 'Is Advertising Still Salesmanship?', *Journal of Advertising Research, 37* (3), 9–15.

McDonald, C. & Ehrenberg, A.S.C. (2003), *What Happens When Brands Gain or Lose Share? Customer Acquisition or Increased Loyalty?* Report 31 for Corporate Members, Adelaide: Ehrenberg-Bass Institute for Marketing Science, pp. 1–2.

Morrison, D.G. & Schmittlein, D.C. (1988), 'Generalizing the NBD model for customer purchases: What are the implications and is it worth the effort?', *Journal of Business & Economic Statistics, 6* (2): 145–59.

Persky, J. (1992), 'Pareto's law', *Journal of Economic Perspectives, 6*, 181.

Romaniuk, J. (2011), 'Are you blinded by the heavy (buyer) ... or are you seeing the light?', *Journal of Advertising Research, 51*(4), 561–3.

Scriven, J. & Danenberg, N. (2010), *Understanding How Brands Compete: A Guide to Duplication of Purchase Analysis*, Ehrenberg-Bass Institute for Marketing Science, p. 12.

APPENDIX: AROUSAL TESTING RESEARCH METHOD EXPLAINED

KAREN NELSON-FIELD WITH HAYDN NORTHOVER

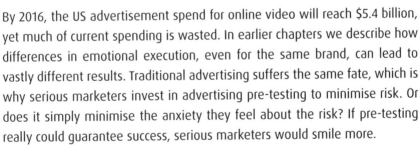

By 2016, the US advertisement spend for online video will reach $5.4 billion, yet much of current spending is wasted. In earlier chapters we describe how differences in emotional execution, even for the same brand, can lead to vastly different results. Traditional advertising suffers the same fate, which is why serious marketers invest in advertising pre-testing to minimise risk. Or does it simply minimise the anxiety they feel about the risk? If pre-testing really could guarantee success, serious marketers would smile more.

Current debate in the field of arousal testing sees self-reporting facing off against biometrics in a battle for measurement gold. While this battle rages, we still need to press on with research, so this chapter discusses how we have measured arousal and why we have chosen our methods. Don't worry: this is not a tedious literature review on pre-testing approaches and their theoretical background. Rather, it reveals what we did to understand how emotions affect sharing.

IN THE BLUE CORNER

There is evidence to suggest that even though self-report and expert panels are commonly used, they offer a fallible pre-testing process (Binet & Field 2007). More recently, with advances in technology, biometrics[1] has taken centre stage, yet techniques central to biometrics, such as skin conductance, facial expression, electroencephalography (EEG) or functional magnetic resonance imaging (fMRI) all have their limitations. Their predictive power has not been validated over many sets of (large) data. For this research we needed a technique that offered a cost-effective measure for large-scale data; yet, at the same time, could minimise errors associated with the subjectivity of emotions measurement.

SELF-REPORTED MEASURE

The primary aim was to understand how sharing is affected by the emotional responses an audience elicits from video content. Consequently, it was necessary to determine which emotional response a viewer may have to all of the 800 videos included in the study. Given the scale of the data and to minimise fatigue, 28 independent coders were recruited. Coders were asked to watch a random subset of videos and indicate which emotions they felt from the list of 16 potential emotional responses. The development of the list of potential emotions was based on the desire to capture both low- and high-arousal and positive- and negative-valence responses. Each emotion was classified based on previous classifications in the literature.

While agreement on what would constitute a negative or positive emotion is easy to reach, the level of arousal associated with particular emotions is notably more subjective. For example, where one person might think a video is 'laugh out loud' hilarious, the other may smirk and think it is merely amusing. Even among academics there is little consensus. For example, Berger and Milkman (2012) classify sadness as a low-arousal emotion, while

---

1   Also referred to as neurophysiological tools, they are the centrepiece of neuromarketing.

Cacioppo et al. (2000) classify it as a high-arousal emotion. Similarly, Berger and Milkman (2012) classify joy as a low-arousal emotion, while Dobele et al. (2007) classify it as a high-arousal emotion.

To limit subjectivity and confusion of terms, the list was developed around positive and negative emotional pairs. Pairs help to add context to the difference between two points of measurement. For example, the definition of surprise is 'the feeling caused by something unexpected' (Cambridge University Press 2013). The definition of astonishment is 'extreme surprise', making it an appropriate high-arousal positive emotional term and a suitable pair for surprise. While other studies have used scales to measure the strength of emotions felt, pairs are considered useful when the underlying scale of measurement is subjective.

> To limit confusion when testing, pairs are useful when the underlying scale of measurement is subjective.

Coders were fully briefed on the concept of arousal and given the dictionary meaning of each emotion. The specific emotions used in the study were drawn largely from the psychology and neurophysiology literature (see Baumeister & Bushman 2010; Rimé et al. 1998; Griskevicius, Shiota & Nowlis 2012; Turner 2007). Table 3.2, earlier in this book, shows the full list of 16 emotions and their classification into positive or negative valence, and high or low arousal level.

To limit the effects of subjectivity, we ensured coders were both unaware of the rates of sharing for each video and blind to the objectives of the study. All videos were then double coded, with two coders watching each and indicating the emotions that they felt in response. In total, 800 surveys were collected for each set of 400 videos. This provided some indication of differences in coding behaviour between coders. There was a high level of inter-coder agreement across both sets of data (average 92 per cent), suggesting that a wider audience would have a similar reaction to the same videos. In addition, the use of a large sample of videos minimised the potential impact that particular coders may have had on the results and implications of the research.

> When coding emotions, using multiple coders can minimise subjectivity.

Important to methodological reliability is that the results were found to generalise across two very different data sets.[2] Replication is a prerequisite to results that can be applied, as discussed in Chapter 2. The obvious implication here is that if the self-reported methodology we used produced the results in one data set by chance, then the likelihood of the results replicating perfectly, and under differing conditions, is very low. Consequently, we consider this method both appropriate for the data and rigorous because of its ability to generalise across data.

BIOMETRICS: THOSE MEN IN WHITE COATS

With all that said, self-report measures still attract criticism, most notably for being simple proxies for underlying and subtle brain activity. Advancement in technology offers the capacity to more directly measure brain activity. The field of biometrics is growing. This is largely due to scepticism of traditional self-report measures—specifically surveys, which can be biased. Biometrics are used by many of the largest companies in the world. Those publicly known to use biometrics in some manner include Hyundai, Google (YouTube), Walt Disney Co., Microsoft, Chevron, PepsiCo, PayPal, Motorola, P&G, Buick, Facebook, Campbell's, 20th Century Fox, Coca-Cola, Unilever, Nestlé and GlaxoSmithKline. In the field of marketing, biometrics and neuromarketing are comparatively new. So, it comes as no surprise that the marketers with

---

2   Actually, the study was conducted a third time on a smaller data set of 40 Super Bowl videos. This data set was introduced mainly for the purpose of recall analysis, but the results relating to arousal and valence were identical also.

the biggest budgets have popped this sexy new measurement tool in their toolbox.

The burning question for this research is: can biometrics help predict subsequent video shares? The answer is that biometrics would only be beneficial if:

- they achieved a higher level of predictive accuracy than the self-reporting method described at the start of this chapter
- a moment-by-moment trace was produced to indicate the level of interest, engagement or arousal for the individual elements of the video (of which self-report is incapable).

In the research discussed in Chapter 3, we found that videos that are coded as high-arousal positive are shared more than any other arousal–valence combination. A difficulty with using biometric measures to test the hypothesis that high-arousal positive videos are shared more is that the definitions of high arousal or positive are not universal among the biometric providers. For instance, Innerscope collects skin conductance (a noted arousal measure; see Bradley & Lang 2000; Bradley et al. 2001), respiration, heart rate and motion, yet doesn't report the individual measures. Instead, they rely on a patented (or patent-pending) algorithm, with the metric termed 'engagement'. Innerscope demonstrated the value of 'engagement' using Super Bowl ads (among n = 30 respondents). They identified the number of online 'views' of the ads on the public online portal MySpace, as well as the number of comments per advertisement. Their evidence demonstrated that their 'engagement' scores were somewhat associated with subsequent video views of Super Bowl ads (r = 0.49) as well as the number of comments (r = 0.62) (see Siefert et al. 2009).

Other providers offering metrics comparable to arousal and valence include:

- Neuro-Insight, which provides a measure of 'emotional intensity', as well as 'approach-withdrawal' (Davidson et al. 1990). Respectively, these are similar to arousal and valence.

- Sands Research, which uses EEG to combine signals from multiple sites—comparable to those used by Neuro-Insight to arrive at an 'engagement' score.
- Affectiva, which uses facial recognition (remote, web-camera) that can distinguish the facial markers of a smile from those of a frown (positive versus negative valence). Algorithms that detect facial expressions are, however, only in their infancy. Affectiva has developed one algorithm to recognise a total of six specific expressions. The algorithm has correctly recognised 64 per cent of expressions, compared with human coders, who coded at 54 per cent accuracy. Using a select group of six basic emotions—anger, fear, surprise, sadness, disgust and happiness—the Affectiva algorithm detected the emotion nine out of ten times. The catch is that they were recognised only when the expression was exaggerated. More subtle facial movements can be reliably classified as 'positive' and 'negative' in three-quarters of cases. Affectiva combines its facial recognition technique with other biometric measures, such as skin conductance, to further gauge how people are responding to stimuli.

As yet, there has been no evidence in the marketing field that links the facial recognition tool and sales effectiveness. However, it is a relatively new tool and further development may provide the link we need. One concern with facial recognition methodologies is that facial expressions of emotions are a communicative tool, hence they are less likely conveyed in the solitary testing environment common in market research. Also, some emotions are present without being observable on the face—think professional poker players. The point is that without testing it is difficult to know whether these issues have any practical significance.

CAN SELF-REPORT BE LINKED TO SALES EFFECTIVENESS?

One self-report mechanism that offers potential is the Self-Assessment Manikin (SAM), which has noted consistencies with skin conductance (Bradley & Lang 2000). Using standardised pictorial stimulus, the more pleasant or unpleasant an item, the higher the arousal. Pictures that elicit low levels of arousal tend to be rated affectively neutral (Bradley et al. 2001).

An alternative self-report measure from Brainjuicer (www.brainjuicer. com) reports that the discrete emotion 'happy' is predictive of sales-effective advertising (Wood 2010). Working on the Paul Ekman principle of seven universal emotions (sadness, disgust, anger, fear, contempt, happiness and surprise), Brainjuicer uses seven faces representing each emotion to display to respondents. Their main measure, 'emotion-into-action', is essentially a measure of the emotion selected by respondents, factoring in the intensity of the emotion felt. This measure, they argue, is better at identifying sales-effective advertising than traditional pre-testing measures, such as 'persuasion' and 'brand linkage'—although, to our knowledge, this hasn't been tested using single-source sales data. As discussed in Chapter 7, we are currently using our coding framework to link emotions to direct sales.

ARE BIOMETRICS BETTER?

They could be if they were able to offer us a moment-by-moment trace of a response to a video. Each biometric tool would need to be tested against the same stimulus. What we are looking for goes way beyond an evaluative score. The ability to trace the fleeting emotional responses to a video would have significant impact on creative direction, content and distribution.

Emotions can be fleeting, with a quick onset and an equally quick dissipation. The ability to track moment-by-moment responses passively would be an advantage over self-reported techniques, which lack sensitivity to the dynamism of emotions. Passive forms of measurement—either biometric or neurophysiological—are better suited to gauge the temporal progress of a social video. For instance, skin conductance measurement will track the arousal levels over the course of the advertisement, while facial recognition can track the level of valence. Likewise, all EEG measures are collected so that they can be represented over time.

Measuring arousal via skin conductance offers a moment-by-moment picture of the communication, yet analysis and interpretation issues still remain. If you were to watch a skin conductance trace in response to an emotive stimulus you would see an increase in the trace two to three seconds after the event, with a slow decline thereafter, until the next emotive event.

In this way, movement in arousal can be tracked. However, each individual has a unique response time; for one person it might be three seconds, and for another it might be two seconds. These differences introduce a level of measurement error. Similarly, fMRI has a slow response and is unable to adequately track response for the same reason. EEG, on the other hand, has a high temporal resolution, meaning that stimulus and response are essentially concurrent.

CONCLUSION

Arousal testing, as with the testing of all subjective criteria, is a contentious field. Self-reporting and expert panels have been criticised for failing to accurately gauge the emotional content of stimulus material, while biometrics are yet to be tested against large sets of data. A well-constructed coding system that displays high inter-coder reliability *and* can predict the level of subsequent video sharing is 'measurement gold'. Biometrics can offer value in understanding how, and when, arousal and valence are displayed. However, further assessment of biometric methods is required to determine whether it can be used for accurate prediction of video sharing.

> A well-constructed coding system that displays high inter-coder reliability *and* can predict the level of subsequent video sharing is 'measurement gold'.

Until then, the self-test method paying careful attention to the coding framework offers a rigorous way to assess the large amounts of data required to obtain generalisable findings. In time, advances in the coding framework may help to assess the moment-by-moment response to a video. This would add a new layer of applicability to the testing method, with a coding system that can be used for diagnostics as well as evaluation.

REFERENCES

ABC News (2012), '"Dumb Ways to Die" creator explains quirky clip', video, YouTube, 21 November, accessed at 2012 at www.youtube.com/watch?v=_H8blstI4w4.

Associated Press (2012), 'Kony campaigner's wife explains "irrational" acts', *Sydney Morning Herald*, 18 March, accessed at www.smh.com.au/world/kony-campaigners-wife-explains-irrational-acts-20120318-1vcwu .html#ixzz1sOO6DOFD.

Baumeister, R. & Bushman, B. (2010), *Social Psychology and Human Nature*, Belmont, Wadsworth: Cengage Learning.

Berger, J. & Milkman, K. (2012), 'What makes online content viral', *Journal of Marketing Research*, *49*, 192–205.

Binet, L. & Field, P. (2007), 'The pursuit of effectiveness', *Market Leader*, Winter, 54–7.

Bradley, M. & Lang, P. (2000), 'Measuring emotion: Behavior, feeling and physiology', in R. Lane & L. Nadel (eds), *Cognitive Neuroscience of Emotion*, New York: Oxford University Press.

Bradley, M.M., Codispoti, M., Cuthbert, B.N. & Lang, P.J. (2001), 'Emotion and motivation I: Defensive and appetitive reactions in picture processing', *Emotion*, *1*, 276–98.

Brehm, S.S. & Brehm, J.W. (1981), *Psychological Reactance: A Theory of Freedom and Control*, San Diego: Academic Press.

Cacioppo, J.T., Berntson, G.G., Larsen, J.T., Poehlmann, K.M. & Ito, T.A. (2000), 'The psychophysiology of emotion', in M. Lewis & J.M. Haviland-Jones (eds), *Handbook of Emotions* (2nd edn), New York: The Guilford Press.

Cambridge University Press (2013), *Cambridge Advanced Learner's Dictionary*, Cambridge University Press.

Carlson, N. (2008), 'Most people don't watch web video for more than 60 seconds', *Business Insider*, 2 December, accessed at www.businessinsider.com/2008/12/people-only-watch-web-videos-for-10-seconds-or-less-?IR=T.

CBC News (2011), '"Your Man" breast cancer video gets million hits', online posting, 3 November, accessed at www.cbc.ca/news/canada/toronto/ story/2011/11/03/breast-cancer-video.html.

Company Films (2012), 'John Grammatico's "Rethink Breast Cancer" PSA wins 2 IAB MIXX Awards', accessed at http://w3.unisa.edu.au/cags/documents/ apceasupportingdocs/harvard_final_jan_2011_may_update%5B1%5D.pdf.

comScore (2013), 'comScore releases December 2012 US online video rankings', 14 January, accessed at http://www.comscore.com/Insights/Press_ Releases/2013/1/comScore_Releases_December_2012_U.S._Online_Video_ Rankings.

Cumming, G. (2012), *Understanding the New Statistics: Effect Sizes, Confidence Intervals, and Meta-Analysis*, New York: Routledge.

Dahl, D., Frankenberger, K. & Manshandra, R. (2003), 'Does it pay to shock?', *Journal of Advertising Research*, *43*(3), 268–80.

Davidson, R.J., Ekman, P., Saron, C.D., Senulis, J.A. & Friesen, W.V. (1990), 'Approach-withdrawal and cerebral asymmetry: Emotional expression and brain physiology', *Journal of Personality and Social Psychology*, *58*, 330–41.

Davis, E. (2011), 'Rethink breast cancer viral video triggers more than a million views in four weeks', *Profectio*, 7 November, accessed at www.profectio .com/rethink-breast-cancer-viral-video-triggers-more-than-a-million-views-in-four-weeks.

Dobele, A., Lindgreen, A., Beverland, M., Vanhamme, J. & Van Wijk, R. (2007), 'Why pass on viral messages? Because they connect emotionally', *Business Horizons*, *50*, 291–304.

'Dumb Ways To Die' (2012), video, YouTube, 14 November, viewed 4 December 2012 at www.youtube.com/watch?v=IJNR2EpSOjw.

Eckler, P. & Bolls, P. (2011), 'Spreading the virus: Emotional tone of viral advertising and its effect on forwarding intentions and attitudes', *Journal of Interactive Advertising*, *11*, 1–11.

Ehrenberg, A.S.C. & Bound, J.A. (2000), 'Turning data into knowledge', in C. Chakrapani (ed.), *Marketing Research: State of the Art Perspectives* (Handbook of the American Marketing Association and the Professional Market Research Society), Chicago: American Marketing Association.

Ehrenberg, A.S.C., Uncles, M.D. & Goodhardt, G.G. (2004), 'Understanding brand performance measures: Using Dirichlet benchmarks', *Journal of Business Research*, *57*(12), 1307–25.

Garfield, S. (2010), *Get Seen: Online Video Secrets to Building Your Business*, New Jersey: John Wiley & Sons.

Gillie, B. (2013), 'Fast-food lover Don Gorske discusses life after 26,000 Big Macs', video, *The Examiner*, 6 January, accessed at www.examiner.com/article/ exclusive-fast-food-lover-don-gorske-discusses-life-after-26-000-big-mac-s.

Griskevicius, V., Shiota, M. & Nowlis, S. (2012), 'The many shades of rose-colored glasses: An evolutionary approach to the influence of different positive emotions', *Journal of Consumer Research*, *37*, 238–50.

Guinness Book of Records (2013), 'Most Big Macs consumed', accessed at www. guinnessworldrecords.com/world-records/dedication/most-big-macs-consumed.

Haley, R.I. & Baldinger, A.L. (1991), 'The ARF Copy Research Validity Project', *Journal of Advertising Research*, *31*(2), 11–32.

Hammer, P., Riebe, E. & Kennedy, R. (2009), 'How clutter affects advertising effectiveness', *Journal of Advertising Research*, *49*(2), 159–63.

Heath, R. (2009), 'Emotional engagement: How television builds big brands at low attention', *Journal of Advertising Research*, *49*(1), 62–73.

Heath, R. & Feldwick, P. (2008), 'Fifty years using the wrong model of advertising', *International Journal of Market Research*, *50*(1), 29–59.

Hennig-Thurau, T., Wiertz, C., Bohnenkamp, B. & Paul, M. (2012), 'What drives consumption and engagement on online media-sharing platforms? An Investigation of YouTube', Conference Proceedings in AMA Winter Marketing Educators' Conference, Las Vegas.

Ho, J.Y.C. & Dempsey, M. (2010), 'Viral marketing: Motivations to forward online content', *Journal of Business Research*, *63*(9), 1000–6.

Huffington Post Canada (2011), '"Hot Man" app from Rethink Breast Cancer reminds women to check their breasts regularly', 21 October, accessed at www .huffingtonpost.ca/2011/10/21/hot-man-breast-cancer-app_n_1023679.html.

Jarboe, G. (2013), 'Super Bowl advertisers can learn lessons from social video trends', *Search Engine Watch*, 14 January, accessed at http://searchenginewatch.com/article/2235942/Super-Bowl-Advertisers-Can-Learn-Lessons-from-Social-Video-Trends.

Johanson, M. (2011), 'GetUp! Australian gay marriage ad "It's Time" goes viral', *International Business Times*, 29 November, accessed at www.ibtimes.com/getup-australian-gay-marriage-ad-%E2%80%98it%E2%80%99s-time%E2%80%99-goes-viral-video-376216.

Jones, J.P. (1995), 'Single-source research begins to fulfill its promise', *Journal of Advertising Research*, *35*(3), 9–16.

Kaitin, K. (2012), Accessed at http://www.bostonglobe.com/business/2012/09/30/mit-professor-andrew-proposes-cancer-megafund-billion-speed-cures/iHLdtvRaOZfgHqFuxjQ7MJ/story.html.

Kennedy, R., Sharp, B. & Rungie, C. (2000), 'How ad liking (LA) relates to branding and the implications for advertising testing', *Australasian Journal of Market Research*, *8*(2), 9–19.

Kinser, J. (2011), 'It's time: The making of a viral video love story', *The Advocate*, 30 November, accessed at www.advocate.com/news/news-features/2011/11/30/its-time-making-viral-video-love-story.

Lodish, L., Abraham, M., Kalmenson, S., Livelsberger, J., Lubetkin, B., Richardson, B. & Stevens, M. (1995), 'How T.V. advertising works: A meta-analysis of 389 real world split cable T.V. advertising experiments', *Journal of Marketing Research*, *32*(May), 125–39.

Luminet, O., Bouts, P., Delie, F., Manstead, A.S.R. & Rime, B. (2000), 'Social sharing of emotion following exposure to a negatively valenced situation', *Cognition & Emotion 14* (5), 661–88.

Malhotra, N.K., Jain, A. & Lagakos, S. (1982), 'The information overload controversy: An alternative viewpoint', *Journal of Marketing*, *46*(2), 27–37.

Mann, R.P., Faria, J., Sumpter, D.J.T. & Krause, J. (2013), 'The dynamics of audience applause', *Journal of the Royal Society Interface*, *10*, 85.

May, C.P., Hasher, L. & Kane, M.J. (1999), 'The role of interference in memory span', *Memory & Cognition*, 27, 759–67.

Moses, A. (2012), 'Aussie viral video, "Dumb Ways to Die", lives on', *Sydney Morning Herald*, 29 November, accessed at www.smh.com.au/technology/technology-news/aussie-viral-video-dumb-ways-to-die-lives-on-20121129-2ahm0.html.

Nalty, K. (2010), *Beyond Viral: How to Attract Customers, Promote Your Brand, and Make Money with Online Video*, New Jersey: John Wiley & Sons.

Nelson-Field, K., Riebe, E. & Sharp, B. (2012), 'What's not to "Like?": Can a Facebook fan base give a brand the advertising reach it needs?', *Journal of Advertising Research*, *52*(2), 262.

O'Brien, J. 2012, 'How Red Bull takes content marketing to the extreme', *Mashable*, 20 December, accessed at http://mashable.com/2012/12/19/red-bull-content-marketing.

On Top (2011), 'Australian gay marriage video "It's time" racks up 3 million YouTube views', 2 December, accessed at www.ontopmag.com/article.aspx?id=10247.

Prinz, F., Schlange, T. & Asadullah, K. (2011), 'Trial watch: Phase II failures: 2008–2010', *Nature Reviews Drug Discovery*, *10*(5), 328–9.

Rethink Breast Cancer (2012), 'Your Man Reminder "The hottest app update ever"', video, YouTube, 11 October, accessed at www.youtube.com/watch?v=3omQdVqRbDA.

Rick, C. (2012), 'Branded video content helps Red Bull find its marketing wings', *ReelSeo*, January, accessed at www.reelseo.com/red-bull-branded-video-content.

Rimé, B., Finkenauer, C., Luminet, O., Zech, E. & Philippot, P. (1998), 'Social sharing of emotion: New evidence and new questions', *European Review of Social Psychology*, 9, 145–89.

Rimé, B., Paez, D., Kanyangara, P. & Yzerbyt, V. (2011), 'The social sharing of emotions in interpersonal and in collective situations: Common psychosocial consequences', In I. Nylelicek, A.J.J.M. Vingerhoets, & M. Zeelenberg (Eds.), *Emotion Regulation and Well-Being: Conceptual and Clinical Issues* (pp. 147–164) , New York: Springer.

Romaniuk, J. (2009), 'The efficacy of brand-execution tactics in TV advertising, brand placements and internet advertising', *Journal of Advertising Research*, *49*(2), 143–50.

Romaniuk, J. (2012), 'Are you ready for the next big thing? New media is dead! Long live new media!', *Journal of Advertising Research*, *52*(4), 397–99.

Romaniuk, J., Beal, V. & Uncles, M. (2013), 'Achieving reach in a multi-media environment. How a marketer's first step provides the direction for the second', *Journal of Advertising Research*, *53*(2), 60–9.

Romaniuk, J. & Hartnett, N. (2010), 'Investigating the relationship between branding execution and advertisement liking in television advertising', in P. Ballantine & J. Finsterwalder (eds), *ANZMAC Conference: 'Doing More With Less'*, Christchurch: Department of Management.

Romaniuk, J. & Sharp, B. (2004), 'Conceptualizing and measuring brand salience', *Marketing Theory*, *4*(4), 327–42.

Scott, D.M. (2011), *The New Rules of Marketing and PR: How to Use Social Media, Online Video, Mobile Applications, Blogs, News Releases, and Viral Marketing to Reach Buyers Directly*, New Jersey: John Wiley & Sons.

Seamon, J. (1980), *Memory and Cognition*, New York: Oxford University Press.

Sharp, B. (2010), *How Brands Grow*, South Melbourne: Oxford University Press.

Sharp, B. & Romaniuk, J. (2007), 'There is a Pareto Law—but not as you know it', *Report 42 for Corporate Sponsors*, Adelaide: Ehrenberg-Bass Institute for Marketing Science.

Sharp, B., Wright, M., Dawes, J., Driesener, C., Meyer-Waarden, L., Stocchi, L. & Stern, P. (2012), 'It's a Dirichlet world: Modeling individuals' loyalties reveals how brands compete, grow, and decline', *Journal of Advertising Research*, *52*(2), 203–13.

Shayon, S. (2011), 'Red Bull, bullish on branded content', *Brand Channel*, 30 August, accessed at www.brandchannel.com/home/post/2011/08/30/Red-Bull-Bullish-on-Branded-Content.aspx.

Siefert, C.J., Kothuri, R., Jacobs, D.B., Levine, B., Plummer, J. & Marci, C.D. (2009), 'Winning the Super "Buzz" Bowl: How biometrically-based emotional engagement correlates with online views and comments for Super Bowl advertisements', *Journal of Advertising Research*, *49*, 293–303.

Szokan, N. & Fazeli-Fard, M. (2012), 'Video on "dumb ways to die" attracts millions of online viewers', *The Washington Post*, 4 December, accessed at www

.washingtonpost.com/national/health-science/video-on-dumb-ways-to-die-attracts-millions-of-online-viewers/2012/12/03/a1fbb290-6964-11e1-acc6-32fefc7ccd67_story.html.

Teixeira, T. (2012), 'The new science of viral ads,' *Harvard Business Review*, *9*(3), 25–7.

Teixeira, T., Wedel, M. & Pieters, R. (2010), 'Moment-to-Moment optimal branding in TV commercials: Preventing avoidance by pulsing,' *Marketing Science*, *29*(5), 783–804.

This Is Not Advertising (2011), 'The Evian Rollerbabies Campaign', 8 July, accessed at http://thisisnotadvertising.wordpress.com/2011/07/08/the-evian-rollerbabies-campaign.

Turner, J. (2007), *Human Emotions: A Sociological Theory*, New York: Routledge.

Unruly (2009), 'Evian—Roller Babies', 9 November, accessed at http://unrulydev.squarespace.com/case-studies/evian-roller-babies.html.

Unruly (2012), 'Viral Video Chart: Dumb Ways to Die', accessed at http://viralvideochart.unrulymedia.com/youtube/Dumb_Ways_to_Die?id=IJNR2EpS0jw.

Unruly (n.d.), 'Viral Video Chart', accessed at http://viralvideochart.unrulymedia.com/all.

Voltz, S. & Grobe, F. (2012), *The Viral Video Manifesto: Why Everything You Know Is Wrong and How to Do What Really Works*, New York: McGraw-Hill.

Watts, D.J. (2004), *Six Degrees: The Science of a Connected Age*, WW Norton and Company Inc. New York.

Watts, D.J. (2012). *Everything is Obvious*, New York: Crown Business, p. 111.

Watts, D.J., Peretti, J. & Frumin, M. (2007), *Viral Marketing For the Real World*, Harvard Business School Publishing.

Wein, D. (2012), 'It's Time', *Huffpost Gay Voices*, blog posting, 21 September, accessed at www.huffingtonpost.com/daniel-wein/gay-marriage-rights-_b_1903359.html.

Wood, O. (2010), *Using an Emotional Model to Improve the Measurement of Advertising Effectiveness*, Market Research Society, Annual Conference, Market Research Society.

Wood, O. (2012), 'How emotional tugs trump rational pushes: The time has come to abandon a 100-year-old advertising model', *Journal of Advertising Research*, *52*, 31.

World Record Academy (2011), 'Most viewed online ad: "Evian Roller Babies" sets world record (Video)', 1 July, accessed at http://www.worldrecordacademy .com/internet/most_viewed_online_ad_Evian_Roller_Babies_sets_world_ record_112346.html.